"Inside The Box" Fair Ministry

Handbook

For Saving Souls &

Training Confident Soul Winners

Dr. Thomas W. Miller

DEDICATION

To Pastor Jeffery Walters, my partner and more importantly my friend, whose vision was the catalyst to this great ministry. Also my wife, Laura, who has edited and made my words sing for the past thirty-one years.

All scripture quoted is from the

Holy Bible, King James Version

CONTENTS

ACKNOWLEDGMENTS

The members of the First General Baptist Church of Waterford, Mi and Charity Baptist Church of Oxford, Mi who support this innovative method of taking the Gospel of Jesus Christ to the masses.

To the Pastors: Mike Stallard, Darrin Lee, Alan Rydman, Gordon Rydman, Tim Charlton, Jeffery Stonerock, Pedro da Cunha and Hardy Smith. These men of God have helped to expand the kingdom of our Lord and Savior through the usage of Inside the Box. Their love of God and trust in this ministry both humbles me and brings joy. I'd like to also recognize the "In The Garden Mission" of Virginia whose members have used the box at different events for the last three years.

Our missionaries, Dr. Bob Hollis, Rev. Craig Logan and the number three man at IBFM, Dana Babka, for their loyalty and faith in God to provide as they seek to expand this ministry.

Our supporting Churches: First General Baptist of Waterford Mi, Charity Baptist of Oxford Mi, Sugar Camp Baptist of Booneville Ky , Victory World Outreach of Goodrich Mi, and Central Baptist Church of Mt. Pleasant Mi. Also Brother Skip Pascouay. We would like to thank all of these for the financial support which has helped us to spread this method of evangelism.

Our crew: Cliff, Dick, Dave, John, Art, Steve and the scores of people who have discovered the greatest passion of all through this ministry - leading people to Christ.

Finally, and most importantly thank you to our Lord and Savior Jesus Christ who gave His all so we could have eternal life. May we be found faithful at His return.

INTRODUCTION

This book examines 21st century America and asks the question, "How can the church reach a society which has become increasingly Bible illiterate?" It also looks at the biblical nature of evangelism, how it began in the streets in Acts Chapter 2 and became more personal and one-on-one in nature in Acts Chapter 8 through present day.

Also examined are different types of marketplace evangelism which use varying methods to attract people to the saving knowledge of Jesus. It focuses on Assembly Line Team Evangelism which is the method used by Inside the Box Fair Ministry.

Over a five year period of time and based on over 6500 salvations, it is shown that Assembly Line Team Evangelism is an effective method to expose Jesus to a lost world. In addition it is also a means to prepare and train a novice Christian in how to soul-win without fear through the use of scripts, tips, and how to meet and answer objections and excuses.

By utilizing and adapting modern applications to soul winning techniques and marketplace evangelism in particular, Inside the Box Fair Ministry can assist churches in not only seeing mass salvations, but to also easily train new soul winners, remove the fear of sharing their faith and bring about a spiritual revival within their congregation.

In the first four years of existence Charity Baptist Church of Oxford, Mi. and First General Baptist Church of Waterford, Mi., who together began Inside the Box, have seen God grow this ministry from one venue a year to eleven and the number saved from 517 the first year to over 6700 as of February 2013. At the time of this writing Inside the Box is hosting annual events in Michigan, Kentucky, North Carolina and Virginia. The first international outreach was in the Dominican Republic in February of 2013 where young ministers at a Bible institute were taught how to lead people to Christ using this technique. Currently in planning stages is a trip to Cuba in January of 2014 to meet with the Cuban Alliance of Baptists to train them to use Inside the Box.

MISSION

The first year of the ministry the primary purpose was to see people saved. As time has progressed, the mission purpose evolved into three objectives:

1. **To bring the lost to the saving grace of Jesus Christ.**
   This is the driving force behind this ministry. Those that serve God through this effort count this more than their meat and more than their drink. As Christ's return becomes more imminent it is important that God's people be found about His business at His return. There is a saying that is continually chanted in our church and to the workers, "we are building a Kingdom not an Empire." In a day and time when success in a ministry is measured by the size of the church, Inside the Box Fair Ministry believes it is the size of His Kingdom in the end that matters.

2. **To work with the local church, training them to use Inside the Box as a soul winning tool.**
   The founding churches of this ministry still work their local fair and technically it is the only fair they 'work.' However, they send out teams to both train and help other churches to work their local events. The founding churches of Inside the Box cannot minister and follow up on people led to the Lord in say, Virginia. But, when Virginia's local church, trained by Inside the Box, sees 100, 200 even 500 people saved through their ministerial efforts, revival breaks out in that church.

3. **Teaching people the joy of leading others to Christ.** *"Therefore with joy shall ye draw water out of the wells of salvation."* (Isaiah 12:3)

Chapter 1

SOUL WINNING IN THE BIBLE

In the book of Acts we see two events that in many ways reflect the world in the time in which the church was first taking its baby steps. The first of these happenings occurred in Jerusalem on the day of Pentecost ten days after the Lord Jesus Christ ascended to heaven. In Acts 1: 15 we read that the number of believers that were in Jerusalem were: *". . .about an hundred and twenty. . ."* (Acts 1:15). On the day of Pentecost these people *". . . were all with one accord in one place. . ."* (Acts 2:1). When,

> *". . . suddenly there came a sound from heaven as of a rushing mighty wind, and it filled all the house where they were sitting. And there appeared unto them cloven tongues like as of fire, and it sat upon each of them. And they were all filled with the Holy Ghost, and began to speak with other tongues, as the Spirit gave them utterance."* (Acts: 2:2-4)

Pentecost was a holy day in the Jewish faith and religious people from all around the world made the pilgrimage to the land of their ancestors (v6) tells us that after the 120 were filled with the Holy Ghost the upper room could not contain them and they went into the streets speaking in unknown languages that no matter what region of the world a person was from they understood what was being said. Peter preached a sermon and *". . .there were added unto them about three thousand souls. . ."* (Acts 2:41).

The second event takes place in Acts 17. Here the Apostle Paul is in Athens awaiting the arrival of Timothy and Silas whom he had left behind in Thessalonica. While there he noticed that the city was (Acts 17:16) *". . . wholly given to idolatry. . ."* By this time in the book of Acts the Jewish opposition which started in Jerusalem with the stoning of Stephen (Acts 8) had now spread throughout the Greco-Roman world. Paul found the people to be as nonresponsive in Athens as they had been in so many other places. When certain of the intellectuals of

Athens, "*philosophers of the Epicureans, and of the Stoicks*" (v18) heard this new doctrine of which Paul spoke, their curiosity was aroused and they wanted to hear more. So ". . . *they* (the philosophers) *took him unto Areopagus,*" (v19) [where] ". . . *all the Athenians and strangers which were there spent their time in nothing else, but either to tell, or to hear some new thing*" (v 20). Then just as Peter in Acts 2, Paul preached a message which most dismissed except ". . . *certain men clave unto him, and believed. . .* [and at least one] *woman*" (v 34).

Further examination of these chapters in Acts shows some similarities:
1. A message was given by an apostle (Peter and Paul).
2. Both messages were given to groups of people not previously having the knowledge of the saving grace of God through Jesus Christ.
3. Each group was made up of both nationals and people of like-minded interests from different parts of the world. Acts 2:6 were religious people, and 17:21 were intellectuals and philosophers.
4. People believed after hearing the message.

However, the numbers of people who received Jesus in Acts 2:41 (3000), was a thousand times greater than the three we know with certainty in Acts 17:34. Why such a big difference? Paul answers this question best in 1 Corinthians 1:23 where he says: "*But we preach Christ crucified, unto the Jews a stumbling block, and unto the Greeks foolishness.*"

The Jews already knew the books of the Law, the prophets and Psalms concerning the coming Messiah, therefore the preaching of the cross and Christ was only a spiritual stumbling block.[1] When Peter used the words of the prophet Joel to show them who Jesus was the stumbling block was removed and many believed. However, in Athens, Paul was dealing with an intellectual people who were curious about what he was saying. They did not have a point of Old Testament reference so what most heard that day was "foolishness" to them and the vast majority rejected the message.

There once was a time in America's history when it could be said that this country was a deeply religious nation. In fact it was once reported that "70-75% of all people who came to the Lord at Billy Graham Rallies were already church members."[2] Like the Jews on the day of Pentecost, the people attending these crusades already knew what the Bible said, they just needed a clear presentation of the Gospel in order to be saved. However, in the 21st century United States, 75% of people between the ages of 13-26 have either never been to church, or have not been to church since they were a young child.[3] The lack of church, the removal of God in the public sector as well as the religion of evolution has caused America to become increasingly more like the intellectual society in Acts 17 than the religious society of Acts 2.

This book testifies how marketplace evangelism, in particular Assembly Line Team Evangelism can be used by the local church to reach the lost in an ever increasing Athenian society.

Chapter 2

HISTORY & TECHNIQUES OF MARKETPLACE EVANGELISM

In Mark 1 after Peter and his brother Andrew were done fishing Jesus came to them and said, "Come unto me and I will make you fishers of men" (Mark 1:16). Jesus was comparing fishing to evangelism. While Peter and Andrew were net fishers, I have spent meant hours fishing with a pole. If you think about it net fishing and pole fishing can be compared to two different types of evangelism. Pole fishing requires a pole, some bait and a desire to catch one fish at a time. When witnessing, through personal evangelism or door-to-door, we are pole fishing for souls. On a Sunday morning, during a crusade, revival or media evangelism we are casting nets for souls.

Another type of fisherman we often don't think about is the shell fisherman. The shell fisherman uses specially designed traps that allow the shellfish to enter but not escape. The crew drops these baited cages to the bottom of the ocean. They are left for a few days as the fishermen drop other traps. If everything goes as planned one-by-one the crustaceans are lured into the cage by the bait. When the fishermen return, in the instance of the common blue crap, they can have as many as 80 crabs in a single trap.[4] This type of cage fishing can be compared to a form of evangelism of which many are not aware, that of "fair or marketplace evangelism."

In fair or marketplace evangelism a prop is used as 'lure' or 'bait.' People are then attracted and led into the tent or booth where they are told of the saving grace of Jesus Christ. A simple definition of 'marketplace evangelism' would be, "whenever the purveyors of Christ's good news go where people are gathered."

Five years ago, God led two pastors to use this type of evangelism through Inside the Box Fair Ministry. In this short period of time Inside the Box has been blessed to see the salvation of over 6700 souls (Appendix 1).

Origins of Marketplace Evangelism

Marketplace evangelism is not something new; in fact you could say it dates back to the book of Acts Chapter 2. The 120 believers, filled with the Holy Ghost, spilled into the streets of Jerusalem on the day of Pentecost (a festival day) proclaiming the good news of Jesus Christ. After the day of Pentecost Acts 2:46 tells us that the disciples of Jesus went to the temple daily, and would repeat this action till the arrest and stoning of Steven (Acts 6 and 7). We see the apostle Paul going to the marketplace in Philippi (Acts 16) and while in Athens he went to the market daily as well as Mars Hill where the philosophers gathered (Acts 17).

As the book of Acts was coming to a close the persecution of the Church became more prevalent with the stoning of Paul (Acts 14), the arrest and beating of Paul and Silas in (Acts 16), the arrest of Jason in (Acts 17), the arrest of Paul at the temple (Acts 21), attempts on his life (Acts 23), and the subsequent prison stays and trials. From the midway point of the first century the first of ten persecutions began during this time period. All but one of the apostles, as well as Mark, Luke and Barnabas would die a martyr's death for the cause of Christ.[5]

In many ways due to persecution, the Church became an underground society from the middle part of the first century to the beginning of the fourth century. Fearing persecution, arrest or even death, evangelism became more personal in nature. One-on-one sharing of the Gospel with family or close friends replaced the days of evangelizing at the temple and marketplace. During the Middle Ages the Holy Roman Catholic Church took charge of evangelism. This made them the official religious representative in every country in Europe and controlling the faith through papal edicts and superstitions. For close to 1200 years evangelism went underground becoming once again secretive and personal in nature.

With the reformation true believers in Jesus became more open about their faith. However, most religion in Europe, even though freed from papal oversight, was still restrictive and state run. It was not until the United States Constitution granted freedom of religion that Americans truly became liberated to share the Gospel with a lost and dying world without fear of imprisonment or execution. Other than street evangelism, the previous 1700 years of sequestered evangelism, born out of fear, is still the way most people share the Gospel. In the latter part of the 20th century people began once again to discover the joy that comes from taking their faith and sharing it with total strangers in the marketplace.

Re-Birth of Marketplace Evangelism

Amazing Grace Ministry

In 1962 an Indiana pastor by the name of Dr. James Gardner started going to regional fairs with the sole purpose of leading people to Christ. In relating his experience Gardner wrote,

> "The beginning was slow with the first year seeing no decisions for Christ. I began the next year using 'props' to attract people to a small booth where I could engage people in conversation in an attempt to determine their 'spiritual condition.' Using these methods I was able to ask the person, 'would you like to see what the Bible says about how you can get to heaven?'"[6]

To His great amazement many did want to know and came to accept Jesus as their Savior. In 1983 Gardner's evangelism effort grew and became known as Amazing Grace Ministry. Between the years 2002-2012 over 200,000 people in all fifty states and six continents have come to know Jesus from his discovery of the 'evangelistic prop.'

The Godmobile

Others would follow the example of Amazing Grace Ministry. In 1988, in Lincoln County, Oregon, two fair evangelists, Andy and Bobby Lue Zedwick, were praying for help in their ministry endeavor. The following year God sent them Paul and Lieselotte Jenkins. The Jenkins brought with them the idea that instead of an evangelism tent or booth they would just put a booth on wheels (Figure 4). Thus the Godmobile Ministry was born.[7]

The Godmobile allows the evangelist to set up and/or change location quickly. Also, it only takes one person to operate. As with Amazing Grace, the Godmobile utilized a prop, in this case a questionnaire, to attract the lost to the transportable booth.

Though different operators use different questionnaires they all revolve around two basic questions and choice of answers.[8]

Figure 1: God Mobile Survey:

Q 1. "Do you believe that you will go to Heaven when you die?*"

_____Yes   _____No   _____Not Sure   _____ I Hope So

Some operators have added the line "if you were to die today"

Q 2.   Why do you believe this?**

___I've tried to keep the Ten Commandments   ___ I go to Church

___I believe in God   ___I'm basically a good person

___ I've done the best I could   ___I've never hurt anyone

___ Other_____

**This question is also phrased to read: "Why should God let you into Heaven?"[9]

Once the questions are answered the person taking the survey is then led through a series of questions and supporting scripture with the purpose of leading them to Christ. Most of the questionnaires are printed in tract form and can be used by both the fair evangelist or as a stand alone tract to lead a person to Christ.[10]

The survey technique has been adapted by different churches and organizations. For example, Emmanuel Baptist Church (General Association of Regular Baptists) of Flint, Michigan uses the following survey (Figure 2). Victory World Outreach (Goodrich, MI) also use a survey (Figure 3).

Enticements are used to get people to take their survey. A drawing for items such as gift cards for I-tunes and Wal-mart are used. By entering the person's name in the drawing assures they will have the personal information for follow up.

Figure 2: Emmanuel Baptist Church of Flint, MI Survey

Religious Questionnaire

1. Do you attend Church Regularly? Yes_____ No_____

2. Are you interested in spiritual things? Yes_____ No_____

3. Do you believe the Bible is completely true? Yes_____ No_____

4. Do you believe that Jesus is the Son of God? Yes_____ No_____

5. Do you believe in heaven? Yes_____ No_____ Not Sure_____

6. Do you believe in Hell? Yes_____ No_____ Not Sure_____

7. Do you agree that there is only one way to heaven?

    Yes___ No_____ Not Sure_____

8. If you were to stand before God and He asked you, "Why should I let you into heaven?"what would you say?

9. May I take a few minutes to show you what the Bible says?

    Yes_____ No_____

10.How can I pray for you?

Figure 3: Victory World Outreach Survey

1.Age Group_____10-20 _____21-30 _____30-40 _____Older

2.Do You Believe in God? _____Yes _____No

3.Were You Raised With Any Church Background? ___ Yes _____No

4.Do You Currently Attend Church? _____Yes _____No

5.Can You Name Four Of the Ten Commandments?_____Yes _____No

6.Do You Know What the Bible Says God Requires for you to go to heaven? ___Faith in Christ ___Good Works ___Belief in God

Child Evangelism Fellowship (CEF)

Child Evangelism Fellowship is a worldwide organization whose three part goal is that every child reached with the Gospel of Jesus Christ, is discipled and brought into a local church. They use different ministries to achieve this goal such as "The Good News Club." This is a five day Vacation Bible School type event that takes place in neighborhood settings such as homes, backyards, schools and community centers. This program is designed to bring the Gospel of Christ to children within their own environment.

Other outreaches used by this organization are a Bible correspondence course for both children and new converts, camping, open-air, and internet ministries all targeting children. In 2011 through their efforts over 10 million children heard the Gospel message of Jesus Christ.

One million of those came to His saving grace through their efforts.[11] One of the means by which they accomplished this is via fair ministry. Space is rented at county fairs and local festivals for the purpose of telling children about Jesus. In 2008, in the state of Michigan, the local Child Evangelism Fellowship chapters were involved in 43 fairs and festivals, sharing the good news with 14,632 children and seeing 1031 professions of faith.[12] Following are pictures of the various chapters' booths and apparatus (Figures 5-7). [13]

The 'bait' used here varies from face painting, balloon art, singing or other attractions to attract children to hear the Gospel.

Since the mid 20th century marketplace evangelism has grown from a few venues to a world-wide out reach.

Figure 4: God Mobile sponsored by Full Gospel Business Men's Fellowship, San Diego Chapter 1881

Figure 5: Child Evangelism Fellowship: Grand Valley, MI Caboose

Figure 5a: Inside the Caboose

Figure 6: So. East, Mi., CEF Booth

Figure 7: CEF Tent Genesee Co. , Michigan Chapter

Inside the Box Fair Ministry

Inside the Box Fair Ministry was started in 2008 by Rev. Jeff Walters (Charity Baptist Church, Oxford, Mi.) and Rev. Tom Miller (First General Baptist Church, Waterford, Mi.). The pair did not invent fair ministry but put an innovative twist on the concept. One Sunday evening Miller heard Walters preach a sermon. During the sermon Walters made reference to a fair ministry in which he was involved as a youth pastor in Ohio. After the service Miller asked if it would be possible to start a soul winning ministry at the local county fair using the technique Walters had mentioned. Walters agreed it was a good idea. As they talked they decided to get a space at the local county fair. Walters agreed to build the needed props. Miller would provide the necessary tent and furniture. Inside the Box Fair Ministry was born.

The primary purpose of Inside the Box Fair Ministry (IBFM) is to lead people to the saving grace of Jesus Christ at local fairs and festivals. The secondary purpose is to train churches and their people to become evangelists in a relaxed, non-intimidating atmosphere.

The equipment or props used in the ministry consist of two boxes (Figures 8 and 9), waist high for the average adult, illuminated on the inside, with a view finder on top of each box and a sign over each box. The first sign reads, "The Question Millions Cannot Answer." The second reads, "The Answer Millions Cannot Question." There are also a tent, tables, chairs, gospel tracts, books containing the gospel of John and the book of Romans, prayer cards and a leaflet titled, "Now What Do I Do?" The tent is staffed with at least one box operator, a promoter and up to six evangelists.

Chapter 3

THE INNOVATION OF INSIDE THE BOX FAIR MINISTRY

What makes Inside the Box Fair Ministry unique? Simply "innovation." Inside the Box utilizes a concept that two Michigan born and bred preachers understood, the "assembly line." Many people believe Henry Ford invented the automobile, but that honor actually belongs to Karl Friedrich Benz who received his first patent for an automobile in 1886.[14]   Ford did not build his first car until 1901, 15 years later. In fact, Ford was not even the first car manufacturer in the city of Detroit. That distinction went to Ransom Olds the creator of the Oldsmobile. Many also believe Ford invented the assembly line but again that was Olds. He put the process to work at his plant in Detroit. With the innovation of the assembly line Oldsmobile went from building 11 cars a week to an annual average of 96.[15]

Why then do people think Ford invented both the car and the assembly line? In 1913 Ford's innovation was a *moving* assembly line; the car moved rather than the worker. With this simple innovation Ford Motor Company was able to increase production building an average of 4800 cars a week (compared to only 205 in 1910) the first year this method was in operation. This not only allowed more cars to be built but also allowed the price of the Model-T to drop from $825 in 1908 to only $360 in 1916, allowing the average American to afford a car.[16] Where people saw Ford as an inventor he referred to himself as an innovator. He took an idea from Karl Benz and through innovation was able to make a car faster and cheaper. He took the idea of the assembly line from Ransom Olds and by changing the part that moved increased productivity by twenty-three fold.

In many ways this is what was used to create Inside the Box – innovation. Living in the car manufacturing belt of Michigan the concept of the moving assembly line was understood and became part of the fair ministry. Like Ford, Inside the Box borrowed an idea and put a new twist on it, an innovation to create Assembly Line Evangelism.

Borrowing from Amazing Grace Ministry with its usage of props and being a vendor at fairs, Inside the Box uses props. They are two boxes with a viewer on top and over each box is a sign (refer to Appendix 2 for design).

The first says, "The Question Millions Cannot Answer." (Figure 8). Inside the box is a one question survey; "If you were to die today are you 100% sure you would you go to heaven?"

The sign on Box #2 says, "The Answer Millions Cannot Question." (Figure 9) On the inside of the second box is the scripture, *"Jesus saith unto him, I am the way, the truth, and the life: no man cometh unto the Father, but by me."* (John 14:6)

Difference From Other Fair Ministries

Inside the Box does differ from other evangelistic efforts which use traditional methods that depend heavily on one-on-one contact between the potential convert and the soul winner. Inside the Box uses multiple people to move the unsaved person toward sainthood. Its soul winning assembly line is made up of four to eight people: the Advance Man, the Barkers, and finally the Evangelists. Each person's job is vitally important in the process and each one is of equal importance in the eyes of God.

Unlike Amazing Grace or the Godmobile, the first thing you will notice about an Inside the Box tent is that you do not see 'God' written anywhere. In fact you would never suspect that the boxes or tent have anything to do with the supernatural. This is by design. A person is less likely to try their guess at the 'Question Millions Cannot Answer' if they think it has to do with anything 'religious.' The next difference is Inside the Box workers are dressed in what they call fair clothes: modest, but casual shirts and pants. Jesus said the believer was to "...[be] therefore wise as serpents, and harmless as doves. . ." (Matthew 10:16). Serpents blend into their surroundings. If the workers wore sport coats and ties it would be a dead give-away that something 'churchy' was going on.

The two boxes are purposely displayed in front of, rather than inside the tent. The wording on the signs above each box is significant, "The Question Millions Cannot Answer," and "The Answer Millions Cannot Question." The word 'million' is important. When people see this word they think 'monetary gain.' In fact a day will not go by at a fair where someone does not ask, "What's the million dollar question?"

Props: The Boxes

Figure 8: BOX #1 at Oakland Co. Fair, Mi.

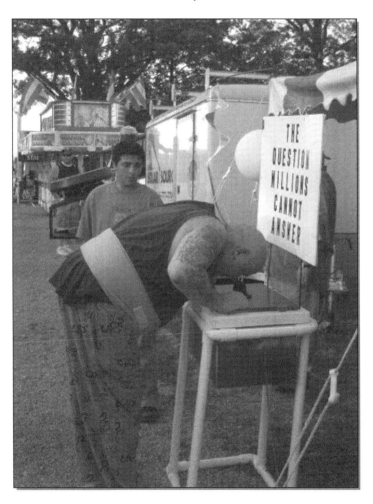

Figure 9: Box #2 at Oakland Co. Fair, Mi.

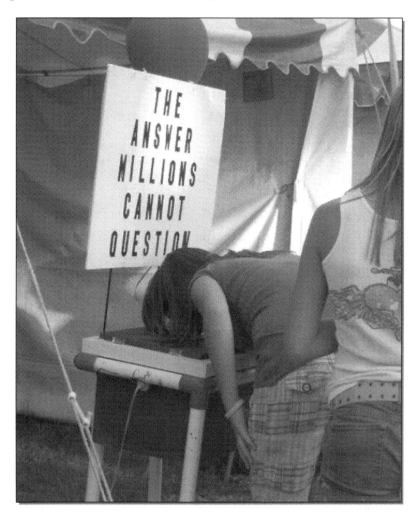

Chapter 4

HOW ASSEMBLY LINE TEAM EVANGELISM WORKS

The fair goer may have received a 'ticket' to look in the box. They will be greeted at the box and moved down the line to the various workers. The workers on the evangelism assembly line are critical to the final product: the new convert. Each plays a role in the preparation. The assembly line team workers are:

--Advance Man

--Barker 1

--Barker 2

--Evangelists (2-6 depending on available space)

Notice that unlike traditional methods of soul winning, which are primarily one-to-one, we use four people to lead one person to the Lord. In this assembly line method while one person is being led to the Lord, the other workers are still able to seek out the unsaved. The Advance Man is still passing out coupons, the Barker 1 is still getting people to come to the box, and Barker 2 is still bringing other people into the tent to other evangelists. The only time when the line stops is when the Barkers are needed to lead others to Christ because the Evangelists' tables are full.

Duties of Workers on the Line

The job description of each worker is briefly stated below, followed by tips and suggestions. There are practice scripts for each worker located in Appendix 4.

Advance Man:

Job Description: Circulate among fair goers on the fair grounds and hand out tickets which are good for a 'free' look inside the box.

Worker Requirement: Energetic, friendly. Teen or adult.

Props: Tickets (Figure 10)

Figure 10:   The Ticket

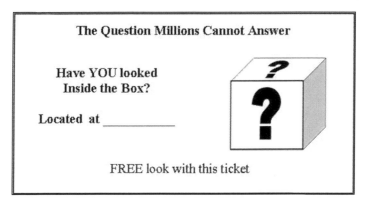

This job is the newest cog in the soul winning assembly line and was originally used at a fair that had a parade. Coupons or 'tickets' (Figure 10) which offered 'one free look' at the 'Question Millions Cannot Answer' were passed out to the parade onlookers. The response was excellent and brought many people to the box. These 'tickets' also became a valuable tool when the placement of the tent or booth was in a less than prime location. As of 2012 the ticket has been used in some form at all fairs and festivals.

The best workers to do this job are teenagers because they usually work the entire crowd, all ages. Children and teens as well as adults will accept a coupon from a teenager. Adults who want to help but are not ready to work the box or the soul winning table are useful in this position. However, adults have a tendency to only give out tickets to people their own age, so they must be encouraged to distribute to all ages. Because most people 30 and over have already made up their mind about Jesus they are more resistant to making a decision in this type of setting. People from the age of 12-30 are more open and curious; they want to know how to get to heaven. Of those that enter the tent, the majority will be between the ages of 12 -30, which makes this the prime target age group. [17] Any person working as the Advance Man will need to be asked to distribute the majority of tickets to this age bracket.

Barker 1 and Barker 2

Job Description: Foremen. Both barkers will man the boxes and invite passersby to 'look inside the box.'

Barker 1 will direct flow between the two boxes, and the activity outside the tent, and kindly discourage 'loitering' that blocks the box whether by workers or fair goers.

Barker 2 will direct flow inside the tent, and escort people into the soul winning tables. Also keep track of all other workers (especially evangelists), coordinate break times and meal times so the soul winning tables are always manned.

Worker Requirements: Zeal for Soul Winning, high energy, friendly, able to work with others and coordinate activities.

Figure 11: Barkers 1 & 2 at Boxes Oakland Co. Fair, Mi.

The word "barker" means "an advertiser of fair attractions.[18] Somebody who stands outside a fair or carnival and shouts out its attractions" Instead of trying to get people to come in to see the tallest man or the bearded lady, the spiritual barker's job is to get people to look inside the box. A tent can operate with just one barker but it is best if you have two who act as a team. (Figure 11) The two are part evangelists, part salespeople, part comics, and part improvisational actors, playing the same routines well over a hundred times on a typical fair day hoping to be rewarded with eternal results. Like the barkers of old this advertising is accomplished through two primary approaches: the Broad Approach and the Direct Approach.

Returning to factory terminology, the two barkers are the foremen of the operation. The Barker 1 is in charge of the operation outside the tent (gets the people to the box, controls flow between the boxes). Barker 2 is in charge of activity inside the tent (keeps track of workers, traffic flow and evenly dividing prospects between the evangelists).

Evangelists (Soul Winners):

Job Description: Soul Winner. Share the plan of salvation. Have Prayer Cards filled out.

Props: Bible, Tracts, Prayer Cards, John and Romans.

Worker Requirements: Must know plan of salvation. Desire to win souls, friendly, good communication skills.

It is the Evangelists' job to share the Gospel and the plan of salvation with the fair goer. Anything that you may say outside the word of God is "your opinion." God is dealing with the unsaved person's heart and that will only work using His Word. Some evangelists use a Bible, others use tracts. As long as the word of God is the focus then either way is good. Whichever way the evangelist feels more comfortable is what they should use, they just need to be well rehearsed.

Figure 12: Evangelist Tables at Virginia Co. Fair

Figure 13: Rev. Jeff Walters at Evangelism Table at Oakland Co. Fair, MI.

Chapter 5

TIPS AND SUGGESTIONS FOR THE WORKERS

Advance Man:

On an average for every 1200 tickets handed out 400 people will redeem them at the box. Out of those 400, 97 will make a profession of faith. The Advance Man must keep in mind that the more people that redeem the cards the more people will be saved.

By handing out 'tickets' and saying, "good luck," you are appealing to a person's flesh. People will literally run to try their hand at answering the question. Quite often at fairs people come by in groups. When approaching a group of young people the Advance Man needs to ask, "Which one of you is the smartest?" Girls have a tendency to point at each other; boys have a tendency to point at themselves. It doesn't matter which one you pick, give them the card and say, "You go over there to the 'Question Millions Cannot Answer,' and tell them (Advance Man's name) said you were the smartest. They will let you all look for free. When you see family groups coming by pick out the youngest in the group.

Appealing to a person's flesh, whether by offering something for nothing, or appealing to their vanity by letting them show how smart they are, is not a sin. Jesus told the woman at the well, *"If thou knewest the gift of God, and who it is that saith to thee, Give me to drink; thou wouldest have asked of him, and he would have given thee living water"* (John 4:10). In this situation Jesus is clearly appealing to the woman's flesh. The Lord did this so that the woman could have a spiritual gain. The fair workers may initially appeal to the person's flesh, but once the person looks in the box everything after that is of their own free will.

The Barkers:

The Barkers need to make what they do as entertaining as possible in order to amuse the passers by. The word "entertain" means: "to engage a person or audience by providing amusing or interesting material."[19] In other words the more entertaining the box workers can be the more the audience may be drawn in. Before a play opens there are many hours of preparation that go into the production. A script is selected, actors are chosen, the set is constructed, costumes are sewn and many hours of rehearsal follow. There is nothing more important in this process than the time spent in rehearsal. When actors are well rehearsed the audience will become part of their world. Being one of God's 'eternal actors' however is different from a stage play. When an actor walks off the stage the play is over, when the Barker leaves 'the box' and brings a person into the tent, a new real life play begins. However, unlike Shakespeare this play can go many different directions.

Every stage play has a director and so does this eternal play. His name is the Holy Spirit and if the workers are prayed up (this cannot be emphasized enough) then the Holy Spirit will direct the workers as if He was speaking through an ear piece. If the Barkers are well rehearsed and able to take holy direction then they will be able to reach the most important person in this play, the lost soul.

The first day of a fair is 'opening night' with all the jitters that go along. Relax. If you are well prepared, and prayed up the Holy Spirit is there to fill in the gaps and give you the words you need.

As mentioned before when large groups are at the box, excitement around the boxes increases. As the Barkers are busy with these large groups the vaudeville rule comes into effect, 'if the first banana cannot perform the second banana takes his place.' In vaudeville the lead comic of the show was referred to as the 'top banana,' many times he was also the emcee. If the top banana could not perform (fell ill, broke a leg, got thrown in jail) then the second banana took his spot and so on. In other words, if you were a comic in an old variety show you needed to be prepared to step into the lead spot at a moment's notice. Every worker in the tent needs to be prepared to do the same thing and be ready to step into the Barker's spot. This happens many times when both Barkers are busy with people and the sudden excitement starts to draw a crowd at the box. The Evangelist needs to keep an eye on the boxes. If they see a backup they need to step out and assume the role as the Barker or which ever job is needed. It is good to train every one at the ministry to work every job.

The Barker also needs to direct the activity outside the tent to insure good traffic flow. It is their responsibility to arrange the tent in such a way that people can easily pass through. However, that is not always easy when a 10' 20' tent gets filled with people. A good way to prevent tent traffic jams is by rotating the active table, keeping aisles clear and pushing in chairs not in use.

A fair can have 100 or more people saved in a day but most of the time these salvations take place in clusters. There may be 30 salvations in one hour and, none in the next three hours. To the best of their ability the Barkers need to evenly divide soul winning time among the evangelists to prevent the evangelists from being bored or wandering off. If they wander they will not be available if a rush happens and souls will be lost.

The Barkers also need to keep track of the Evangelists. In down times workers have a tendency to wander. The Barker needs to have the cell phone number of all the workers on speed dial in case a rush takes place. Also if a worker is going to eat, use the facilities or just take a break, they need to check out with the Barker

The Barker should be aware of the special performance schedules at the fair or event. For example: at the Oakland county fair in Michigan there is a circus that performs at 1:00, 3:00, 5:30 and 7:00 PM adjacent to where their tent is located. The Barker knows that at twenty-five minutes after the show start time there will be a rush of people leaving the event. That is when the tent needs to be manned to the fullest. Explain to your workers that if they are not there to share the Gospel, then people may miss an opportunity to be saved.

The Evangelists:

Prayer is essential to success at the soul winning tables. The Holy Ghost will provide the words to say when you need them. Remember, though, when God gives someone the privilege to be His aide in the act of a person's salvation, it is never the evangelist the person is reasoning with, it is God, through His Word. In this process it is always important to remember the words of our Lord as spoken through the prophet Isaiah: *"Come now, and let us reason together, saith the LORD"* (Isaiah 1:18a).

Also, if a person rejects the Gospel message, they are rejecting God, not you. Do not be discouraged or take it personally. *"And the LORD said unto Samuel, Hearken unto the voice of the people in all that they say unto thee: for they have not rejected thee, but they have rejected me, that I should not reign over them* (1 Samuel 8:7)."

Figure 14: Rev. Miller working as Barker at Oakland Co. Fair, MI.

Chapter 6

EVANGELIZING THE UNSAVED

When fair goers respond to the 'Question Millions Cannot Answer,' it is interesting to note that the correct answer of "because I know Jesus as my personal Savior," or "because I have accepted Jesus as my Savior," is the number sixth answer received. The common order of responses:

1. Because I'm a good person.
2. I do good things.
3. We are all God's creation.
4. I go to Church.
5. I'm awesome.
6. Because Jesus is my Savior.

If the person gives the leader the wrong answer the leader simply asks one last question, "Do you want to know the right answer?" This is the moment of truth; it is at this point you either have them or you don't. If they respond in the positive the leader takes the lost person to the next stop on this moving assembly line which is to one of four or five "evangelist tables each manned by an evangelist." He introduces the curious soul to the "evangelist" who will present the gospel message, the leader then returns to their post at the box. There are many different methods to present the good news of Jesus some of which will be presented later in this work. It is important to know that once inside the tent there has been a remarkable 80% success rate in the fair goer say the sinner's prayer.

Once the person comes to know the Lord they are asked to fill out a prayer card, (Figure 15) which has a place for prayer requests and personal information is gathered. . Having a prayer card provides three things: a means of follow-up, helps to keep count of those who come to the Lord, and gives a name to pray for of the new converts and their needs (even if only the first name is given).

NOTE: it is illegal to gather personal information from children under the age of 14 without consent of a parent

Figure 15: Prayer Card

PRAYER CARD
(Please fill in so we may pray for your needs)

Name_____

Address_____

City_____Zip_____

Phone_____

Email_____

Special Prayer Requests_____

_____

_____

_____

_____

Figure 16: Boxes at Frederick Co. Fair, Virginia (Note tent and evangelist tables behind boxes.)

Chapter 7

Incorrect Reasons People Think They Are Going To Heaven

When a person's response to the question in the first box is "yes" or "I think so," the Barker then asks a second question, "If you were to stand before God and He were to ask you, 'Why should I let you into my perfect heaven?' what would you tell Him?" Sometimes this question is asked after the person has just looked into Box 2 which has the scripture, *"Jesus saith unto him, I am the way, the truth, and the life: no man cometh unto the Father, but by me"* (John 14:6). Yet even when they have just read the scripture most people still answer wrong. In fact, the only right answer which is 'Jesus is my Savior (or any variation thereof), is not even in the top five responses to why a person thinks they are going to heaven.

The Barker will usually respond by saying, "Well, that's a good answer, but it's the wrong answer. Do you want to know the right answer?" For most people this will prick their curiosity and they will answer in the affirmative. However, some will want to know why their answer was wrong. If they do, the Barker will say, "If you give us three to five minutes we can show you, from the Bible, why your answer is wrong and what the right answer is." Most of the time people will go into the tent where the Evangelist can go into the plan of salvation. There are those rare occasions where the person will push for more explanation as to why their answer is wrong. Workers should acquaint themselves with the incorrect responses and related scriptures below. At least once a day they are needed.

Top Five Responses After Looking In the Box

Listed below are the top five responses Inside the Box has received from people who have been asked, "If you were to stand before God and He were to ask you, 'Why should I let you into my perfect heaven?' what would you tell Him?" Following are the biblical reasons why their responses are wrong and the proper response box workers or evangelists give.

1. "Because I'm a good person." Being good is important, but if being good could earn your way into Heaven it would be in violation of God's word, *"For by grace are ye saved through faith; and that not of yourselves: [it is] the gift of God: Not of works, lest any man should boast* (Ephesians 2:8-9). Salvation is a gift of God, not a reward earned for being good.

2. "I do good things." (Give to charity, volunteer time, nice to others, etc.) Again, refer to this scripture, especially the last part, *"For by grace are ye saved through faith; and that not of yourselves: [it is] the gift of God: Not of works, lest any man should boast* (Ephesians 2:8-9). Before you are saved you could do every good work in the world, but it means absolutely nothing. No eternal reward is received.

3. "We are all God's creation." (God made me, so He'll save me.) We are all created by Him, but, we are not all His children, *"But as many as received him* [Jesus], *to them gave he power to become the sons of God* [children of God], *even to them that believe on his name"* (John 1:12). In order for a person to receive the eternal inheritance they must first become a child of God by *"believ[ing] on the Lord Jesus Christ, and thou shalt be saved"* (Acts 16:31).

4. "I go to church." Important, but falls into the category of works (refer to No. 2). It is interesting to note that in the five years since Inside the Box began, 20% of all salvations have been by people who attend church and yet have never made a commitment to Jesus. These people should not be seen as brothers or sisters in Christ until they can give you the right answer. Also, never ask a person if they have received Christ as their Savior until after you have gone through the plan of salvation and have offered them the opportunity to say the sinner's prayer. Just because a person goes to church or has said a prayer in the past does not mean they are saved or that they fully understand what it means to be saved.

5. "I'm awesome." (I'm cool; I'm pretty or any other self glorifying answer.) Most of the time this answer is given when a person is in a group and does not know the right answer. They say the first thing that comes to mind, which is to glorify them. If the box worker were to then ask them, "So you're saying you would go to heaven because you are who you are?" The reply would most likely be *'yes.'* This response in many ways tells us the state of the person's soul.

Although many would say this is simply an off-hand remark, Jesus said, *"...those things which proceed out of the mouth come forth from the heart and defile the man"* (Matthew 15:18). If a person assumes they are going to heaven because they are who they are, what they are saying is, "I'm going to heaven because I am a god." Self worship does not get a person to heaven.

Figure 17: Oakland County Fair, Michigan Evangelist's Table

Top Nine Excuses

Whether at the box or in the tent people have excuses why they will not commit to the Lord or do not think there is a need. What follows are some examples of excuses used by fair goers and a suggested response that can be used by workers to defuse the person's predetermined notion(s) and lead them to the Lord.

1. "I Go to Church" The best response is for the worker to say something like, "I go to church twice on Sunday, once on Wednesday and just about every time the doors are open, but all that will not get me into heaven. Do you want to know what does?" Many people attend church, but as Jesus said, "*Not every one that saith unto me, Lord, Lord, shall enter into the kingdom of heaven. . .*" (Matthew 7:21). The question is not 'do you go to Church?' the question is 'are you born again?' For as Jesus said, "*...except a man be born again, he cannot see the kingdom of God*" (John 3:3).

2. "I've never done anything *that* bad" or **"Everyone that's good goes to Heaven."** The Bible says "*. . . all have sinned and come short of the glory of God. . .*" (Romans 3:23) so let me ask you, how many lies does it take to be a liar? (The answer is of course one.) Follow up by asking the question, "Have you ever lied ?" When they say 'yes' then point out that they *have* sinned. The Bible tells us: "*For whosoever shall keep the whole law and yet offend in one point he is guilty of all*" (James 2:10). Now say, "Being good does not get you into heaven, do you want to know what does?"

3. "I'm not ready to accept the Lord." Workers frequently hear this and a good response is, "Can you show me your expiration date?" When they look at you with a bewildered expression say, "Can you tell me the exact date and time that you know you will die?" When the person says 'no,' tell them of someone you personally know of who has 'died before their time.' At the 2012 Oakland County Fair in Michigan, one of our workers told a fairgoer about her brother-in-law who was waiting to turn left into his driveway. Another car slammed into his car's rear end forcing him into on-coming traffic and killing him instantly. He was only 49. After hearing this story the young woman accepted the Lord, sadly, the young man did not respond, but his lighthearted attitude had changed. In 2011, in Fredrick County, Virginia, 8 young people, some still in high school, some just out, were killed in an automobile accident just before the fair. When a fair goer would say that they weren't ready to accept the Lord, the worker would look them in the eye and say: "I bet you know one of the young people that died recently? Don't you want to make sure if it happens to you that you'll go to heaven?" Isaiah said, *"Seek ye the Lord while he may be found, Call upon him while he is near"* (Isaiah 55:6).

4."You don't know what I've done. God could never forgive me."
Satan has planted these lies into the hearts of people for so long they have begun to believe them. The worker has the opportunity to share the truth with these misled souls. A good response is, "So you are saying God is a liar?" When they say 'no' share with them,

> *"The Lord is not slack concerning his promise, as some*
> *men count slackness; but is longsuffering to us-ward,*
> *not willing that any should perish, but that all should*
> *come to repentance."* (2 Peter 2:9)

Now ask the person, "Are you a somebody?" When they say 'yes' show them Romans 10:13, *"For whosoever shall call upon the name of the Lord shall be saved."* Then ask, "Are you a 'whosoever?'" When they say 'yes' simply say, "Do you want to know what the Bible says about how you can be 100% sure you will go to heaven?"

5. "I'd have to give up too much." This usually comes when the person has a sin issue in their life of which they are not ready to quit. For these people they know,

> "to find God and to accept Jesus Christ would be a very
> inconvenient experience [and] would involve rethinking
> . . .their whole outlook on life and the readjustment of
> [their] whole manner of life." [20]

Most of the time the person is right. Do not ask what the person thinks they will have to give up if they accept the Lord. Deal with the statement not the specifics. It is for the Holy Spirit to convict them of their personal issues/sins not you.

1) point out that the basis of Christianity is faith not sacrifice. It is by faith that a person is saved, *"For by grace are ye saved through faith..."* (Ephesians 2:8). It is by faith that we accept God for who He is and that we can have a relationship with Him through His Son Jesus Christ.

2) the worker needs to let them know that God is seeking *them*, not what they have. God doesn't want a person's possessions, money or even habits. He wants a relationship. *"...for I seek not yours, but you: for the children ought not to lay up for the parents, but the parents for the children. . ."* (2 Corinthians 12:14). If God is then our heavenly Father, it is not what a person has to give up, but more about the abundant blessings He, the parent, wants to give.

6. "The Christian life is too hard (I know I'm still going to sin)." To try to live a holy life is hard but Jesus said, *"For my yoke is easy, and my burden is light"* (Matthew 11:30). When a person comes to the Lord, Jesus is there to bear their burdens and to give them the answers to life's toughest questions. By saying His burden is light Jesus is saying it is not that difficult to follow him.

7. "I can't understand the Bible." The non-believer does not understand the Word because their eyes are not open to the Word. Isaiah, speaking of God, says, *"They have not known nor understood: for he hath shut their eyes, that they cannot see; and their hearts, that they cannot understand"* (Isaiah 44:18). However, God said, *"Come now, and let us reason together, saith the LORD: though your sins be as scarlet, they shall be as white as snow; though they be red like crimson, they shall be as wool"* (Isaiah 1:8). The worker should let the unbeliever know that God wants to show them, through the guidance of the Holy Spirit, how they can have salvation and understand His Word. Now ask, "Do you want me to show you how?"

Stay on track. Keep in mind you are there to lead them to the Lord not to teach them to read the Bible.

8. "I believe everyone will go to heaven." The Bible states,
> *"And [Jesus] went through the cities and villages, teaching, and journeying toward Jerusalem. Then said one unto him, Lord, are there few that be saved? And he said unto them, Strive to enter in at the strait gate: for many, I say unto you, will seek to enter in, and shall not be able."* (Luke 13:22-24)

When Thomas asked Jesus how they would know the way, Jesus responded, *"I am the way, the truth, and the life: no man cometh unto the Father, but by me."* (John 14:6)

After showing the unsaved person these scriptures the worker should tell them, "Now, I am going to show you what *is* needed in order for a person to be saved." From there take them through the plan of salvation.

9. "It is too late for me to be saved." Suggested response: *"For whosoever shall call upon the name of the Lord shall be saved"* (Romans 10:13). The worker should then ask the fair goer, "Are you a 'whosoever?'" When they say 'yes' ask them, "Does it say you *might* be saved? *Could* be saved? Or *shall* be saved? That includes you."

Two important tips to remember when dealing with excuses:
1) Your answers should be short.
2) Stay on track. If a person wants to debate you, or if you cannot answer their question say politely, "Let's get back to that in a minute. Right now let's continue what we started." Then after they have received the Gospel, answer their other question, or if you don't know the answer, tell them you will get back to them with the answer. Have them fill out a prayer card with their contact information.

Chapter 8

TRAINING CONFIDENT SOUL WINNERS

The method below is how Inside the Box has successfully trained over 130 first-time soul winners to lead a combined total of over 6000 to salvation. If the trainee has a love for the Lord and a desire to win souls this system builds confidence and is not complicated or difficult. Everyone who wants to learn how to lead someone to Christ is encouraged to be part of Inside the Box Ministry.

To prepare, all fair workers are encouraged to memorize five verses from the book of Romans which are commonly known as the Romans Road:

Romans 3:23:
For all have sinned, and come short of the glory of God

Romans 5:8:
But God commendeth his love toward us, in that, while we were yet sinners, Christ died for us.

Romans 6:23:
For the wages of sin is death; but the gift of God is eternal life through Jesus Christ our Lord.

Romans 10:9:
That if thou shalt confess with thy mouth the Lord Jesus, and shalt believe in thine heart that God hath raised him from the dead, thou shalt be saved.

Romans 10:13:
For whosoever shall call upon the name of the Lord shall be saved.

The novice can use a well written gospel tract as a script. (The scripts at the end of this paper can also be used for practice training.)

Once at the event a trainee should sit with an experienced evangelist for observation. They do not need to interact, just listen. Depending on personalities and style, they can choose who they feel comfortable sitting with and/or even listen to more than one evangelist. Because of the simple techniques used most trainees feel ready after seeing just one or two people or groups led to the Lord.

As the Evangelist feels the person is ready or the trainee says they are, notify the Barker. The Barker should try to send over a 'soft pitch,' a child or children. This better assures that their first effort will be successful. The experienced Evangelist can either sit with the trainee or be close by if needed.

If the trainee is unsuccessful the first time the Evangelist should compliment them on what they did right and lovingly tell them what to try the next time to overcome any stumbling block. The trainees should not be faulted or told they were wrong. They should be reminded that when a person chooses not to come to the Lord they are not rejecting them as a person, they are rejecting God. Also, that what they are doing is exactly what God wants them to do.

When training a new church, Inside the Box Fair Ministry brings three people: two Barkers and an Evangelist trainer. As the event gets started two of the group will spend the vast majority of the time training new soul winners. After the first day just one will train people, after the second day usually the people are confident to do the work on their own.

If a person shows up to the fair without advance preparation and wants to know how to lead someone to Christ have them sit with an Evangelist and begin training. Just like salvation there are no prerequisites to becoming an evangelist, simply a willingness to lead others to Christ.

New soul winners bring excitement to the tent. Refer to final Discussion section for testimonies from first time soul winners trained by Inside the Box.

DEALING WITH THE SOUL WINNER'S FEARS

When sharing the good news of Jesus the biggest fear people have is the fear of rejection. This is a common fear throughout humanity. We stay at a job we hate fearful that we will be turned down for the job we truly want. A man will pine for a woman and never ask her out on a date in fear that she will turn them down. IBFM shows people how to lead others to the Lord in a non-confrontational environment. With an approximate 80% success rate the fear of rejection soon disappears.

There are several things to keep in mind about managing fear when sharing the gospel:

1. Jesus commanded the believer to *"go ye into the world and preach the gospel..."* (Matt. 28:19-20). This command was so important that he repeated it in each gospel and the book of Acts, Mark 16:14–18, Luke 24:44–49, John 20:19–23 and Acts 1:4–8.

2. Fear or worry shows a lack of faith in God. I think it was no accident that twice the disciples were in a boat or on the water when Jesus showed them the need for faith over fear. First in Matthew 8, when on a crossing of the Sea of Galilee a storm arose while Jesus was taking a nap. The disciples were filled with fear and woke up the master saying, *"...Lord, save us: we perish."* Jesus arose and gave them a loving but stern rebuke, *"Why are ye fearful, O ye of little faith?"* (Matthew 8:25-26). Why do people not believe He will be with them when they cast out in the sea of life to go fishing for men?

The fearful believer must always remember that fear is not of God, *"For God hath not given us the spirit of fear; but of power, and of love, and of a sound mind"* (2 Timothy 1:7). If the spirit of fear is not of God then there is only one other source that it can be from: Satan. A person who is afraid to share the gospel is yielding to the will of Satan and not God. Fear at times may seem as great as a mountain but Jesus said that mountains may be moved with just the smallest of faith, *"...If ye have faith as a grain of mustard seed, ye shall say unto this mountain, Remove hence to yonder place; and it shall remove; and nothing shall be impossible unto you."* (Matthew 17:20) When a person thinks they cannot lead another to Christ they are showing a lack of faith in the power of God, in the words of God and in the Son of God who said with just a little faith, *". . . nothing shall be impossible unto you."* (Matthew 17:20).

3. God will provide the means to lead others to Christ: The fearful believer must also remember that when they go to share the Word they are not alone in their efforts. They have the Word, without which no one can be saved. It is important that scripture be the source of all presentation of the gospel. God says, *"Come now, and let us reason together, saith the LORD: though your sins be as scarlet, they shall be as white as snow; though they be red like crimson, they shall be as wool"* (Isaiah 1:18). It is the Word of God the unsaved reasons with, not the worker. When the soul winner realizes that it is not what *they* have to come up with, but what God has already laid out in His Word the pressure is lessened and fear is relieved.

4. When leading others to Christ the believer is never alone. *"But the Comforter, [which is] the Holy Ghost, whom the Father will send in my name, he shall teach you all things, and bring all things to your remembrance, whatsoever I have said unto you"* (John 14:26). The Holy Ghost will give you the words to say when you need them. The soul winner needs to take comfort in the fact that it is through the Holy Spirit that Jesus' last words in the great commission are fulfilled, *"...I am with you alway, [even] unto the end of the world. Amen"* (Matthew 28:20).

With a salvation success rate of close to 80%, once a new soul winner enters the Inside the Box tent their fear is quickly replaced by confidence. That confidence will continue with the new evangelist for the rest of their life, whether inside the tent, at future events, or in their everyday world.

DEALING WITH OPPOSITION

Whenever you are presenting the gospel Satan will make sure you have opposition. Always keep in mind *"Ye are of God, little children, and have overcome them: because greater is he that is in you, than he that is in the world."* (1 John 4:4) You will encounter many forms of opposition whether dealing with the ministry itself, event management, or even fellow Christians. Never make a scene. Even if the situation is upsetting remember the scripture, *"be ye angry and sin not."* (Ephesians 4:26)

1. Opposition can come from ignorance. For example, in 2011 at the Oakland County Fair in Michigan a parent complained to management because we gathered information (name and age) from her child. We were unaware it is illegal to gather *any* personal information from someone under the age of 14 without permission of a parent. An apology was made and although we continued to lead those under 14 to the Lord we stopped taking personal information from them. Know the rules and abide by them.

Read your contract: Most contracts outline rules of what you can and cannot do. If the contract says you must stay within the perimeters of your space, then do not go out into the aisles or street to bring people in. If it is not specified in the contract then assume you can do it. If it is not in the contract and they allow other vendors to do something, than you may also.

For example, with passing out coupons or free tickets, most event contracts do not say vendors cannot pass out coupons. However, one year when a church was told they could not pass out coupons outside their booth an argument resulted in the closing of their booth. In this particular situation a simple, "We're sorry, we didn't see that in our contract. If you say we can't do this we will stop," would have eliminated the problem. Never forget you are there at the pleasure of the event planners and as such may have to endure some bullying. Also, never forget you are representing our Lord and Savior Jesus Christ. How you behave in these situations will be seen as favorable or unfavorable to the world.

2. Do not invite opposition by debating. For example if a person says they are an atheist you can shake their hand and say with a smile, "I praise God that I live in America where you have the right to be wrong." Most of the time this will defuse any hostility the unbeliever has toward Christians. Even though atheists will accuse Christians of being intolerant, in reality most of the time it is the atheist that is confrontational. Do not try to convert them. Satan has sent them to try to keep you busy with them instead of winning souls. Remember time you spend debating could mean someone loses the opportunity to meet Jesus.

3. Parents often are the biggest opposition. The greatest number of complaints does not come from unbelievers but people of other faiths, in particular Roman Catholic parents. If their child accepts the Lord very often when a Catholic parent finds out they complain to fair authorities. They are usually fearful we are trying to 'convert' their child. The best thing to do in this situation is to start at the box and invite the parents and fair authorities to look inside. Explain that you are not there to make people a Baptist, Presbyterian, Pentecostal or even Catholic. You are there to make sure everyone that comes in the tent will know they are going to heaven. Then ask the parent, "Don't you think that's a good thing?" If you are upfront with everyone and they see you have nothing to hide usually the person with the complaint will apologize.

4. Tourists at the Box. Although this is not really opposition it is a distraction from your priority of winning souls. These are people, perhaps from the host church, who come out to the fair, not to work, but to see what is happening. These people have a tendency to either congregate in the tent or stand outside blocking the view of the boxes. Host pastors do not want to offend them and are hesitant to ask them to leave or move out of the way. The two Barkers have to work in tandem in dealing with these onlookers. If people gather in the tent Barker 2 needs to quietly ask them to take their conversation outside the tent so they do not disturb those who are being led to the Lord. Outside the tent Barker 1 needs to assign a spot for them to converse or watch. For example: if people are standing in front of the box it blocks the view. If they stand half way in the road it diverts traffic away from the box. Barker 1 can strategically locate these people to the box's advantage by arranging their position to flow traffic toward the box.

5. Doctrinal Debaters. Catholics want to debate if Peter was the foundation of the church; Apostolics want to debate the gifts of the Spirit; some believers want to debate creation; others want to discuss when the Rapture takes place; others just like debating. However, if you take time to debate you take time away from winning souls. If someone is standing at the box discussing church politics, they are blocking the box from the unsaved. These are suggested ways to handle the debater:

Rule 1: Do not argue or allow a scene to happen in front of the box. If the person insists on remaining until they get an answer simply move over to the side but inform them you are still 'working' and may have to walk away at anytime.

Rule 2: If the debater still isn't satisfied try asking these seven questions:
1. Do you believe that there is one God who is made up of three parts Father, Son and Holy Ghost?

2. Do you believe that the Bible is the infallible word of God?
3. Do you believe that Jesus came to earth in human form, born of a virgin, lived a perfect life and died for our sins?
4. Do you believe that he rose from the dead and became the first fruit of the resurrection that awaits all believers?
5. Do you believe that Jesus then ascended to heaven so that He can intercede for all believers?
6. Do you believe that the universal church is the collective body of believers past or present who found salvation from Hell and the assurance of Heaven through believing on Jesus Christ?
7. Do you believe the Holy Spirit indwells all believers?

If they say 'yes' to all seven questions shake their hand and say, "Praise God, then we agree on the seven fundamentals of the Christian faith. I've got to get back to work." Then simply walk back to your box. If they say 'no' to any of the questions, shake their hand and say, "Let's agree to disagree. I've got to get back to work." You may have to go some place where they won't follow you, inside the tent, or take a bathroom break.

Rule 3: It takes two to argue - don't be one of them.
Keep in mind that the other person believes their walk with the Lord is the right one. So even if you argue you won't change their mind. Also, remember you are not there to make people Baptist, Pentecostal, Methodist, Catholic or any particular denomination. You are there to introduce the lost to the saving grace of Jesus Christ. Arguing doctrine is counter productive.

Also in the tourist category is the believer who just likes what you are doing and wants to ask questions. Depending on traffic, sometimes you can spend time with these people. (Keep in mind Inside the Box has grown primarily through word of mouth.) These people need to be led to the side, so they are not blocking the box and one of the Barkers can talk to them while the other works the boxes. Explain to the person that you are working and may have to excuse yourself at any time.

Finally, remember, never brag about what you are doing; Praise God for what He is doing.

Chapter 9

THE EFFECT ON THE LOCAL CHURCH

In the first 50 years of First General Baptist Church of Waterford's existence the annual salvation rate was around 21 people, for a 50 year total of 1025 salvations.[21] In just the first two years our church worked the fairs with Inside the Box Fair Ministry that 50 year grand total was more than doubled. By partnering with other churches over the next three years we were also able to partner with God in seeing 6717 salvations. At the old pace, it would have taken 327 years to reach that mark.[22]

It is interesting to note that there was also an increase in salvations outside of the fair ministry. They increased from the previous average of only 21 a year to 43 a year between 2008-2012. I believe this is a reward from the Lord and because our parishioners became emboldened in their faith, and more willing to participate in salvation outreaches. Inside the Box worker Laura Miller stated,

> "I had led people to Christ before in one-on-one situations. After the first fair I worked I was sharing Him with much more confidence with everyone, friends, strangers calling the church asking for assistance, and even phone solicitors."

The after effect in the lives of people are also amazing. In July of 2011, a man came by the tent and told workers he accepted the Lord at our tent the previous year. He went home and told his wife that they needed to start going to church. Since then his wife and his son were also saved and were attending church. In August of 2012, a security guard told fair workers that after accepting the Lord the year before he had stopped drinking and although traveling with the carnival made it hard for him to attend church he spent time in prayer everyday and read his Bible.

In October 2012, Pastors Tom Miller and Jeff Walters while working the Woolly Worm Festival in Beattyville, KY, had the privilege to work the tent with two young ladies who had accepted the Lord one year earlier at the same festival. Pastor Alan Rydman of Mt. Pleasant, MI. writes: "We continue to rejoice, follow up, and see more people saved as a result of [Inside the Box's] ministry here."

Chapter 10

DISCUSSION & RECOMMENDATIONS

A.H. Strong's definition of a local church reads,
> *"a unit of believers who come together voluntarily in accordance with God's law, at a specific location with the purpose of establishing the kingdom within themselves and within the world."*[23]

Our church has a saying, "we are building a Kingdom not an empire." We do not look at the mega church down the road and compare its large congregation to our smaller size. That would distract us from building God's Kingdom. Inside the Box Fair Ministry has helped us to build His Kingdom and at the same time, help our church to become Kingdom focused.

While preparing this book I read Gene Mims' *The Kingdom Focused Church.* I realized after reading it that Inside the Box Fair Ministry has transformed our church into a Kingdom focused church. Mims writes that when a church makes the Kingdom of God its focus three things will take place,

1. Numerical Growth
2. Spiritual Transformation
3. Ministry Expansion through World Wide Missions[24]

The church that I am privileged to pastor, First General Baptist of Waterford, Michigan, has experienced spiritual transformation in the lives of many of its congregants. The annual revival has gone from four days of meetings to six or seven days because there is an increased spiritual fervor. Another example of this spiritual growth is our people's willingness to be part of 24 hour prayer vigils. At one time it took a lot of effort to fill all the time slots. Now when a prayer vigil is announced on Sunday morning people will stand in line to sign up.

The desire to be closer to God is seen not just in worship and prayer but also in their willingness to give to God's work. Since 2008 the church has sent all our teens to camp just through member donations. The opportunity arose to send Inside the Box to the Dominican Republic, but funds were needed. In just a few weeks donations totaling $3200.00 were made and allowed us to send three workers there. In addition there has been an 18% increase in tithes and offerings (even during a recession).

Mims also talked about Ministry Expansion through World Wide Missions. At our church missions giving had dropped to a low of only $1200.00 in 2008. After we began Inside the Box, and I believe, because of the spiritual excitement it generated, our mission giving increased each year. Last year the total World Wide Mission giving was $7550.00 an increase of 600%.

Since beginning Inside the Box Ministry we have witnessed spiritual growth, an increase in missions giving and also in tithing, but as of yet we have not seen an increase in overall church attendance. Which brings us to this point: church growth does not take place because a church participates in a fair ministry; it grows because it is in God's purpose and timing. In his seminar on the Kingdom focused church, Mims stated that if a church focuses on expanding the Kingdom the three things mentioned earlier will happen, but in "what order that takes place is up to God"[25]

Cornerstone Baptist Church (Farmington Hills, MI) and Sugar Camp Baptist Church (Booneville, KY) have both grown numerically since participating through their local festivals. Only three new people came to their church as a result of the Box ministry, but their overall attendance increased. Both churches not only have plans to continue with Inside the Box, they both plan to expand beyond just one festival by working in other venues. They have learned, like us, that God rewards the faithful.

As mentioned in the introduction 75% of people 13-26 are not attending church and as such are not hearing about Jesus. It has become necessary for churches to go beyond their four walls to fulfill the great commission. Inside the Box Fair Ministry is a tool we are using to successfully do just that.

In this increasingly Bible illiterate world, much like Athens in Acts 17, Assembly Line Team Evangelism has proven to be an effective means to reach this skeptical generation. The next question to answer is "How does Inside the Box work in a religious society as seen in Acts 2?"

In February 2013 a group of us went on a mission trip to the Dominican Republic. Working with Iglesia Bautista Cristian in Santa

Domingo, we took the box to the streets. The Dominican is a heavily Roman Catholic culture, so much like the Jews in Jerusalem at the time of Christ, they are very 'religious.' The first day when we worked the box for one hour in front of a department store 57 people were saved. Two days later in front of the Mormon Training Center for the Caribbean, only one hour was spent because the rains came, but 27 were saved. On the final Saturday of our mission trip 30 nationals we had trained accompanied us to the sea shore. We set up the box and in two hours we saw 150 people saved. In four hours it was up to 234. Since leaving the Dominican the young people have taken the box back out more than once and they have seen souls saved each time.

During the five years of its existence Inside the Box has trained over 130 people to share the Gospel of Jesus Christ with others. Debbie Knotts of Winchester, Virginia, doubted the effectiveness of Inside the Box. She wrote after working just three days at the Frederick County Fair,

"I want you to know all doubt is gone. I am humbled by the way God can use an ordinary person like me to do extraordinary things for Him. I had never led anyone to give their life to the Lord until Monday night. Now I can tell you that I cannot count on all of my fingers and toes how many people the Holy Spirit has saved by speaking through me....I now know that Jesus can use me to populate His heaven. If you have the desire to be a doer of the Word and not just a Hearer...I encourage you to step out in faith and try the 'Inside The Box Ministry.' IT WILL CHANGE YOUR LIFE!"

Debbie's husband, Allen, wrote, "I was one of those who had never led anyone to the Lord, but that all changed Monday, praise God. . . I will never be the same after this week."

Dana Graham of Isabella County, MI., writes about overcoming her fear in sharing the Gospel after getting help from Inside the Box worker, Dana Babka,

"...Bro. Dana talked to me after I had sat at a table and tried to witness to some folks and been "shut down." I was discouraged (to say the least). He encouraged me by saying that these folks aren't rejecting you. They are rejecting God. "You have done what you were commanded to do... "Go and Tell!" and they rejected Him." Thank you to the men of the "Inside the Box" Ministries. Thank you a thousand times a thousand, for coming and sharing with us this useful tool that we may in turn, use it to the Glory of God."

Inside the Box Fair Ministry, an innovative assembly line team evangelism method, works at fairs, one day festivals, church events and, as we saw in the Dominican, even just where there is a lot of foot traffic. Wherever people are it can be used. It works in secular communities as well as religious third world countries. It is also the perfect tool to use to train confident soul winners.

Keys to Success
There are two things most important to the working of Assembly Line Team Evangelism. First is prayer. Without sufficient prayer success is limited to human ability instead of God's power. Prayer needs to cover everything, from registering for the event, to setup, the event itself, the workers and weather and even the breakdown. A 24 hour prayer vigil prior to the fair is also a suggestion. During an event when traffic or salvations have slowed, prayer has changed things when a pair of workers went out onto the midway to pray. There have been times so slow yet stopping to pray has sent a spiritual cloud into the tent and a wave of new salvations. Also dividing up the completed prayer cards between the workers and having them pray over them keeps the focus on reaching the lost. Praying for the 'young girl's brother who is in prison.' or for the 'boy who just lost his mother,' or the 'grandpa who has cancer' serves as a reminder to the worker that there is a hurting world out there that needs Jesus.

The second key is the person in the Barker position. Energy level is important. Their personality should be fun and lively as well as loving toward the fair goers and passionate for the Lord. Like a good pastor or sales manager the Barker's job is to keep the morale and motivation of his work force high. Any lackadaisical attitude by the barkers will be reflected in the tent.

Keeping Count
People will ask, "Why count?" In Acts Chapter 2 and 4 they counted the number of souls saved. Numbers were recorded when Jesus fed the 5000 and the 4000. There is a Biblical concept behind

counting. Every denomination asks for an annual report from their churches, of which the numbers of conversions are part. Most churches give annual reports to their parishioners, of which the numbers of salvations are a part.

Counting is also sound business practice. It lets us know from year to year how we are doing. If numbers drop at a particular event we can examine what took place and how to address it the following year. We can also help others churches to avoid obstacles or cope with a situation such as weather or bad location.

Counting brings excitement to the tent. Workers are a little more charged if they know they are about to reach a goal, (30 saved in an hour, 100 saved in the day, going for a new daily record). In fact the barkers need to continually keep track of the numbers so they can use them as motivational tools.

Counting helps peak curiosity. The expansion of Inside the Box Fair Ministry has primarily been through word-of-mouth. What peaks a pastor's or church's interest is not that 'a lot of people' got saved at the Genesee County Fair, but that 'over 600 people' got saved at the Genesee County Fair in just a week. People may not believe it, but they become curious. If a pastor becomes interested, then they may accept an invitation to come observe.

The one question that always seems to be on everyone's mind is; "How many of those people are *really* saved?" My response is this,

> "the only person this side of Heaven that I can truly say is saved is me. I cannot save anyone. That is God's job. My job is to present the Gospel."

Inside the Box Fair Ministry has, in the last five years, presented the gospel of Jesus Christ to over 6700 people who responded by saying a pray of commitment. We are not out to get notches on our spiritual belts, nor is our goal eternal rewards. Our goal is to present the Gospel to a lost and dying world.

Factors Affecting Success

With the exception of the Oakland County fair in Michigan every fair or festival worked had a drop in numbers the year(s) following their first event. There are many factors affecting this: Weather, Attendance, No longer new, Lack of workers, Location and Lack of Prayer.

Weather or the 'Goldilock's Syndrome': If it is too hot people do not respond; if it is too cold people do not respond. We discovered in Michigan that the weather in which people best respond is 75-85° degrees with low humidity. Also rain plays a big factor. Just like a baseball game, event days can get rained out. The second year of the Genesee County Fair in Michigan had 2 days rained out which included a tornado sighting. On hot days we discovered that handing out tickets, and/or offering a bottle of water if people looked in the box, increased traffic tremendously. Also, at the Woolly Worm Festival in Kentucky, which is in October, offering coffee and hot chocolate along with water helped when the temperature dropped.

Overall Attendance at Event: If attendance is down at an event because of weather, as in the heat wave of 2012, there's not a lot you can do about it. Just be prepared to take advantage when the weather breaks.

No Longer New: In successive years, you don't have the novelty factor. Many people have already seen you. Trust that God still will bring reward to your faithfulness.

Lack of Workers: The third year of the Genesee County fair key workers were missing; one couple moved, one man had surgery and still another couple's work schedule changed. Numbers went down. Workers will come and go, so it is important to continually train new people. Also a new soul winner in the tent brings new and new life in the tent brings new souls to the Lord. Also, a lack of female workers limits the 'friendly' factor. A tent full of older men trying to appeal to a teenage group may not be perceived as 'wholesome.' Women add a level of credibility and safety to the appearance. They are important in the evangelistic arm of this ministry.

Location of Space: Being exiled to the worst spot on the fair grounds does affect numbers. If the location is bad then printing out twice as many tickets to hand out and offering simple incentives (bottled water) can help. Early registration for the following year and requesting a change in location are encouraged.

Lack of Prayer: In any endeavor the importance of prayer cannot be over emphasized. Satan is a roaring lion and soul-winning is a spiritual battle. Spiritual armor must be worn. Failure to be prayed up can result in poor attitudes, fatigue, conflict, disruptive influences by weather, fair employees, fair-goers, and even well-meaning visitors. Pray without ceasing.

Chapter 11

EXPENSES

The one-time start-up costs are minimal, involving construction of the boxes, purchase of tracts and a tent or canopy. Whenever possible donations of equipment and supplies should be sought, including a tent. The first years of Inside the Box the tent and/or canopy were donated. It was only this last year that canopies were purchased.

Many variations of the boxes and signs have been used. On the low-end was a sturdy cardboard box, painted, with a hole cut in the top (to look through) and sides (for natural light to enter). These only lasted for a short time duration. The most popular and sturdy boxes have been made from PVC pipe. The PVC frames and plywood boxes with electric light inside have made it through several years. Refer to Appendix 1 for pictures and details of the boxes. They can be easily constructed the cost for the PVC style is around $100. The signs themselves should be professionally made to make the most impact and to withstand the weather, cost is from $20-30.

Each festival or event has a space rental fee. Refer to Appendix 2 for a detailed accounting of Events and their fees for space rental. Most county fair events include one or two free parking passes for vendors. At the local county fairs workers rode to the event together to save gas and additional parking costs. If others came out later by pre-arrangement they parked at a nearby church and were then shuttled by those with the parking pass that day. Scheduling was important to make sure the box and tent were always manned.

When just getting started it is best to use what you have and borrow what you need, this helps minimize the initial costs. Once the first harvest of souls is in you will not hesitate to make further investments in this marketplace ministry. Another option is to contact Inside the Box ministry. They may be able to provide equipment and training crews for your inaugural event to help you get started and get the most out of this type of soul winning.

Suggested equipment and items necessary to operate are listed in the following pages. Many can be borrowed if funds are not available. Make sure borrowed items are labeled and returned to their owners.

Figure 18: People waiting to 'Look Inside the Box' in the Dominican Republic

One Time Expenses

Tent: Needed, a 10x20 tent that opens on three sides or two 10x10 popup canopies. (This all depends on the size of the space.) Which is best for your needs? The tents are best for extended fairs because they are staked out and are less likely to blow away in bad weather especially when you are not there. Another advantage of using a tent at a multiple day event is the ability to zip it up at night; this simple security measure keeps people from roaming through your tent when you are not present. For festivals the popup canopies are the way to go; each one goes up with only two people in less than three minutes. At a one day festival the canopy will be attended the whole time so you don't have to worry about it blowing away. Watch for end of season sales to find the best prices.

Tables and Chairs: Begin with what you have or can borrow. Most churches will have chairs and tables readily available. Quantity will depend on size of the tables; smaller tables are easier to accommodate in the tent. Figure out how many chairs and tables your space will accommodate. Inside the Box (Oakland County) purchased six lightweight 2x3 "Tailgate" aluminum tables for less than $100. These have worked out the best and in the three years we have used them only one needed to be replaced. Old wooden chairs were donated, but cushions are needed for all day sitting. Metal folding chairs work well; cost is about $25 per new chair. Some evangelists may choose to bring their own more comfortable chair.

Do not forget the extension cords (Two or three 100 ft cords - depending on where your power source is located), power strips, and hanging lights are a must if your event goes into the evening hours. Also large fans at least two; one for inside the tent and one for the box workers.

Recurring Expenses:

Tracts/John & Romans: Some tracts can be obtained for just the cost of shipping and handling from any number of places on the internet. John and Romans can also be obtained just for shipping and handling fees for those who donate to "Bearing Precious Seed" which is a print Bible ministry.[26] A plastic, lidded tub is suggested to store these in overnight.

Hydration, hydration, and more hydration is a must on hot summer days. Make sure you have lots of cold bottled water for the workers.

If your event does not offer electricity, an alternative source of power can be obtained by using a car battery and an AC/DC power converter. Both can be purchased for between $100-150.00. This will provide all the power you need in a day.

Refer to Appendix 4 for a suggested list of equipment and supplies.

Accept Donations

Tell your church members what is needed to make the ministry successful. Do not doubt their generosity or deny them the blessing of giving. During a particularly hot summer, it was found that fair goers were disinterested and unwilling to stop for a look in the box until a free bottle of cold water was offered if they looked. The church members were eager to be a part of the ministry by donating cases of water, not just for the workers but as incentive to have people look in the box. Members were also willing to bring bags of ice.

At Goodrich, Michigan's Festival in the Park (one day event), Victory World Outreach passed out 400 bottles of water and cans of pop if people would look in the box. 102 people were saved in one day. (That figures out to 1 salvation for every 4 bottles of water handed out.) If a church wishes to give beverages away to everyone that looks in the box a good way to offset this expense is to have parishioners buy a case of water every time they go to the store. This was done by the Sugar Camp Baptist Church (Booneville, KY) at the Wooly Worm Festival. Members brought cases of water to church in the weeks leading up to the festival. Only two additional cases of water were needed.

Meals are expensive at fairs and festivals. It is left to the workers to buy or bring their own lunches. Providing a cooler and ice for their lunches and beverages is a good idea. If your contract allows, purchase of or borrowing a small grill (propane) allows for fixing fresh food at your space. Church members are also usually willing to donate packaged snacks and some have even provided sandwich fixings that can be kept in a cooler.

APPENDIX

1-Salvations Summary

2-Box Design Plans

3-Expense Summary

4-Equipment & Supplies

5-Scripts for Workers

6-Leaflet: What Do I Do Now?

APPENDIX 1: Salvations Summary By Year & Event

Year/Event	Days	Salv	Yr Tot.
2008			
Oakland Co. Fair	7	527	**527**
2009			
Oakland Co Fair	7	517	**517**
2010			
Genesee Co Fair, MI	7	612	
Oakland Co Fair, MI	7	512	**1124**
2011			
BkPk Hnd out, Fenton, MI	1	25	
Clothing Outr, KY	1	20	
Foundr's Fest, Farmtn Hills, MI	3	226	
Frederick Co. Fair, VA	7	237	
Genesee Co. Fair, MI	6	500	
Oakland Co. Fair, MI	6	507	
Wooly Worm Festival, KY	3	289	**1804**
2012			
Bk Pk Hndout, Fenton, MI	1	50	
Foundr Fest, Farmt Hills, MI	3	115	
Frederick Co Fair, VA	7	140	
Genesee Co. Fair, Flint, MI	7	367	
Goodrich Festiv, MI	2	102	
Isabella Co Fair, MI	6	583	
Oakland Co Fair, MI	10	551	
Ortonville Fest, MI	1	100	
Vict. Wrld Teen Evt	Mo'ly	45	
Wooly Worm Festival, KY	3	230	**2283**
2013 Jan & Feb only			
Dominican Republic	5	460	**460**
5 Year total (as of 2/28/13)			**6715**

APPENDIX 2: Box Design Plans

Over five years there have been several variations of this design, everything from a sturdy cardboard box to this PVC design complete with an old viewmaster in the top and a light on the inside.

This basic box stand (pictured on the next page) consists of 2" PVC pipe, 3 way tees and 2 way elbow joint fittings.

The frame of the box has a large sign at the back. (This particular box uses a wire frame and a sign made from foam core.)

The upper part of the stand supports 'the box' which is made of light weight wood with a hinged top. Inside the box is a light and the

Questions. Each question is printed on white paper and placed in a plastic sheet protector inside the box.

Box 1: "If you were to die today are you 100% sure you would go to heaven?"

Box 2: "Jesus saith unto him, I am the way, the truth, and the life: no man cometh unto the Father, but by me." John 14:6

See Picture on following page.

Appendix 2a:**PVC Box Construction (Viewed from Rear Side)**

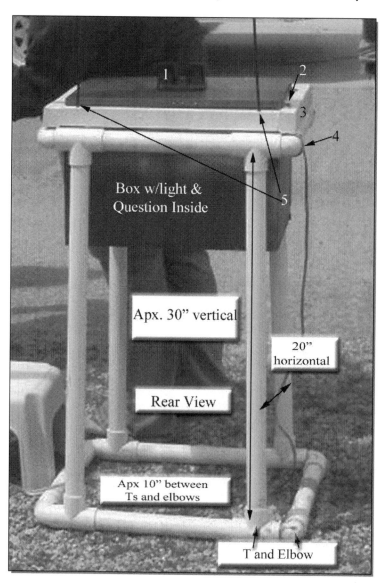

Box w/light &
Question Inside

Apx. 30" vertical

20"
horizontal

Rear View

Apx 10" between
Ts and elbows

T and Elbow

Key on page following

Appendix 2b: **Key to PVC Box Construction (previous page)**

1 Viewmaster set into top of box.

2. Hinges for box lid

3 The box has a frame built around the top with 2x2s. When set into the PVC stand, this frame sits over the top of the PVC to hold the box in place.

4 Hole for Electrical Cord for low wattage light bulb.

5 Two holes are drilled into the 2x2 to insert the legs of the wire sign frame into.

All measurements given are approximated

The signs on these boxes were supported with a PVC frame.

Appendix 3: Expense Summary

2008 – 2012 (International Dominican Trip NOT included)

Year/Event	Rental	No.Days	Salvations
2008			
Oakland Co. Fair	$532	6	527
2009			
Oakland Co Fair	$532	6	517
2010			
Oakland Co Fair	$532	6	512
Genesee Co Fair	$650	7	612
2011			
Oakland Co Fair	$532	6	507
Genesee Co Fair	$650	7	500
Frederick Co, Va	$210	2	237
Fest, Frmg Hills, MI	$200	2	226
Clothing Outr, KY	0	1	20
Fenton, Mi Church Ev	0	1	25
Wooly Worm, KY	$200	3	289
2012			
Oakland Co Fair	$590	10	551
Farmt Hills, MI	$200	2	115
Isabella Co Fair, MI	$250	5	583
Frederick Co, VA	$210	5	140
Genesee Co Fair, MI	$650	7	367
Goodrich Fest., Mi	$100	1	102
Church Evt, MI	$0	1	50
Ortonville Fest, MI	$100	1	100
Vict. Wrld Teen Evt	$0	1	10
Wooly Worm, KY	$200	3	230

5 Yr Total Expenses (2008-12) $ 6338.00   (86 days)   6255 salvations

To break this down to a few statistics:

Average Cost Per Day $ 6338.00 / 86 days = $73.69

Average cost Per Soul $ 6338.00 / 6255 = $ 1.01

Average Souls saved Per Day   6255 / 86 = 72

APPENDIX 4: Equipment & Supplies Used (Based on a 6 Day Fair)

Essentials (Borrow whenever possible or ask for donations
2 Boxes w/Signs
1 Tent or Canopy (10x20 total size)
4-6 Tables (suggested 2x3)
4 Chairs per table
1000 Prayer Cards
1000 Tickets Per Day that say "Look Inside the Box"
1000 Tracts with church name & contact
1000 John & Romans
144 Pencils/pens
3 Fans
5+ Extension Cords (100 ft depending on power source)
1-2 Power strips
1-2 Hanging Flood Lights for night events (one per table)
2 cases of Bottled Water per day for workers (based on 8 workers)
1 Large Insulated Cooler
10# Ice per day

Extras that have been useful
First Aid Kit (bandaids, headache remedies, antacids, etc.)
Tarp to cover equipment at night
Storage Tubs w/lid
Propane Grill
Wet wipes
Paper Towel

Workers Should Bring Their Own
Bible
Bug Spray
Sun Block
Hat
Sunglasses
Lunch/Snacks

APPENDIX 5: Scripts for Assembly Line Workers

William Shakespeare starts his play *"As You Like It"* by making the statement, "All the world's a stage, and all the men and women merely players."[27] Each person has a part to play in inviting a person into the tent. Keep in mind people have come to the fair to have fun (that's why most traveling carnivals have the word 'amusement' in them). Following are a few scripts that can be used as outlines or blueprints for inviting people to look inside the box.

NOTE: These scripts are not intended to be memorized. They are to be a guide or plan to help you rehearse and become comfortable with your role.

Advance Man

Adv Man   "Have you looked at the 'Question Millions Cannot Answer?'"

Fair Goer   "No."

Adv Man   "Here's one free pass to give it a try, good luck."

When you see family groups coming by pick out the youngest in the group:

Adv. Man   "Hi, what's your name?"

Fair Goer   "Billy."

Adv. Man
(Tom)   "Hi, Billy, I want to give you this card.. Take it over there and tell them Tom said you were the smartest in your whole family. They will let you look at the 'Question Millions Cannot Answer' for free.

In these situations the child makes sure the family gets over to the box.

Barker

It is best if two barkers are working the box at the same time. This allows for a wider variety of interaction between the fair goers. The tandem method can also be a little more entertaining to the by passers and stimulate interaction and curiosity.

The Broad Approach:
The barker just shouts out to everyone who passes by, with such lines as
--"How about it? Have you looked in the box?"
--"Step right up and see if you can answer the 'Question Millions Can Not,' and it's free."

The Direct Approach:
The direct approach is aimed primarily at the target age group of 12-30, one person at a time. The lines from the broad approach can be modified to use in this more direct application, for example:
--"Young man, have you seen the 'Question Millions Cannot Answer?'"
--"Young man come here, have you looked in the box yet?"
--"Hey you, come here, go ahead, take a look"
 Both approaches have been proven equally successful and the one the barker uses will be the one he feels most comfortable with. In either approach, after the person has looked in the box the barker will ask, "so, what's your answer?"

YES Answer to the Question:

If the answer is, 'I think so,' or 'Yes,' he sends them to the barker at the answer box. After they have read the answer in Box 2, the barker will ask, "Does that match your answer?" If it does then smile and say, "God Bless you."   If they are with a group and have friends who did not know the answer the Barker should ask, "You want your friends to know, don't you?" Refer to the "Go Team" section on pages 70-71.

NO Answer to the Question:

If the answer is 'no' or 'I don't know,' the barker simply asks, "Do you want to know?" If the response is 'yes,' the barker takes them into the tent (If there are more people waiting at the box or if the person is with a group, the barker hands them off to the leader).

Who's The Smartest?

Barker 1:   "Which one of you are the smartest?" (At this point a mock argument arises between the two box workers.)

Barker 2:   "I think the guy in the blue shirt is the smartest."

Barker 1:   "Well I think the guy in the red shirt is the smartest. Help us settle this, see which one of you can answer the question inside this box."

The mock argument can be used when people are just passing by.

Who's The Smartest 2

Barker 1:   "I say the girl in the white blouse is smartest."
Barker 2:   "Nah, anyone can clearly see the girl in the glasses is the smartest. Hey, girls can you help us settle an argument?"

Barker 2:   "I say that you can answer the 'Question Millions Cannot Answer' and he says she can. Let's show him who's smartest."

The Friendly Wager
IBFM does not endorse betting of any kind however, as time has passed the box workers have discovered that people will have a greater tendency to look in the box if they think a person is helping someone win a bet. It starts out with the mock arguments above then follows with the lines:

Barker 1:   "Whoever guesses the greatest number of smart people by the end of the night the other has to buy him dinner?"

Barker 2:   "Yeah, I bought him dinner last night, but he's going to buy it for me tonight, because I said you (pointing at one of the fair goers) can answer the question inside this box."

Barker 1:   "I say that you can answer the 'Question Millions Cannot Answer' and he says she can. Let's show him who's smartest."

[Disclaimer: when working a fair Pastors Jeff and Tom never keep count of who guessed who was the smartest so they declare their wager a tie and bring their own lunches.]

Go Team!!
When there are groups of four or more the two barkers can divide the people into two teams. This is done for several different reasons.
1. It creates excitement around the box the more excitement around the box the more people will be curious about what is going on and will want to look in the box.
2. It's fun for those that are participating.
3. When they are taken into the tent to be evangelized they are already in smaller groups making it easier for the evangelist to handle.

This method starts like this:

Barker 1:   Which one of you are the smartest?
(Most of the time in a group of 4 or more two people will raise their hands, when this happens Barker 2 jumps in.)

Barker 2:   I see a challenge, ok, let's divide into teams. You're first captain," (pointing at one of the people who raised their hand) "you're second captain" (pointing at the second person).

Barker 1:   Whichever team has the most people that can answer 'Question Millions Cannot Answer' wins. Team one goes first.

Barker 1:
At this point the barker takes his station at the question box and the leader takes his station at the answer box. Because you have two

groups, whether the answer given is yes or no you send each person of Team One to the answer box, then it is Team Two's turn. After each person answers the question the barker keeps that team at the question box. In both situations the leader and the barker ask the same questions,

Q 1: "How many of you said yes?" After a show of hands the second question is asked.

Q 2: "If you were to stand before God and He were to ask, 'why should I let you into my perfect heaven?' What would you tell Him?"

Any answer that does not have' Jesus' in it is wrong. The Barker then says,

Barker: "Do you want to know?"

The group is then invited into the tent to hear the right answer.

If one person in the group knows the answer (is saved) the barker will say,

Barker: "You want your friends to know, don't you?"

By asking the question this way the friend becomes part of the lost person's salvation. In fact they often become the motivating force to get the lost person(s) into the tent.

Evangelist

IMPORTANT NOTE: Do not automatically ask if the person is 'saved' or if they ever said the sinner's prayer. So many people will say yes to both, yet they still are not sure if they will go to heaven. Somewhere the communication has broken down. They are either not committed to the Lord, not going to church to build on their knowledge and faith, or were not truly saved.

It is important to take them through the full plan of salvation. When you come to the point of inviting them to say the sinner's prayer if they say they have already done that, then ask, "Are you sure you are saved?" If the answer is 'yes' ask if they would like to rededicate their life to the Lord. If the answer is, 'I'm not sure I'm saved,' ask, 'Do you want to be sure?' Then lead them in the sinner's prayer.

Make the assumption that anyone coming before you needs to know Jesus as their personal Savior.

If questions are asked that you are not sure how to handle, do not hesitate to call upon another person to assist. Also Review Chapter 5, "Tips and Suggestions."

Evangelist:	Hi, I'm Tom, and you are...?
Fair Goer 1	I'm Joe, this is Glen.
Evangelist	So you weren't sure if you were to die today that you would go to heaven?
Joe	That's right.
Evangelist:	Let me start out by asking you if you know what a sin is?
Glen	Isn't that when you do something wrong?
Evangelist:	Well, it's not just that. It is whenever you do something that is displeasing to God. (Showing the fair goer Romans 3:23) 'All have sinned and come short of the glory of God.' So does that mean that you're a sinner, Joe?
Joe:	Yes.
Evangelist:	Does that mean you're a sinner Glen?
Glen:	Yes.
Evangelist:	And I may go to church every time the doors are open but you know what? I'm a sinner too. That's a problem because I want you to look at this verse (Romans 6:23) 'For the wages of sin is death...' Do you know what a wage is?
Glen:	Isn't that when you get paid?
Evangelist:	That's right, a wage is payment for something you

earned. The payment for our sin is death. Now, this is not physical death, we all will physically die. The death mentioned here is spiritual death. Physical death by definition is "absence of life." This word from the Greek means "separation from God."[28] Do you know how bad the world is today? (wait for response) Can you imagine how bad it would be if God was not here?

Joe:

It would be pretty bad.

Evangelist:

That's right, this existence is what the Bible refers to as Hell and that's a place none of us want to go. Jesus said Hell is where the "...worm (he is speaking of man here) dieth not, and the fire is not quenched. (Mark 9:44)" And that's what we have all earned because of sin. But let's keep reading (show Romans 6:23) 'but the gift of God is eternal life through Jesus Christ our Lord.' That gift is salvation through the Lord Jesus Christ. Do you know how sin entered into the world?"

Glen:

I'm not sure did it have to do with Adam and Eve?

Evangelist:

That's right; God told them they could eat of any fruit in the Garden of Eden except from the tree of the knowledge of Good and Evil on the day that they would eat of it they would die. Well they ate of it and the two of them are not alive today because of it. Well because of their sin God kicked them out of the Garden, and killed some animals for their hides to cover Adam and Eve's nakedness or sin. God provided the first sacrifice for sin and from that point on he required man to make sacrifice for sin because the scripture tells us "...without shedding of blood there is no remission of sin" (Hebrews 9:22). So people would sacrifice sheep, doves, bulls or whatever they could afford and once a year on the day of atonement they were to bring their sacrifice for sin to the temple. Do you know how long that sacrifice was good for?

Joe: A year?

Evangelist: No. It was only good until they sinned again. From that point they needed another sacrifice to be forgiven. So God, who provided the first sacrifice, also gave mankind a gift, the perfect sacrifice, His son, Jesus Christ, that through Him all sin could be forgiven for all time." But that is only for those who accept that free gift. I want you to read this verse with me,

Together: (Romans 10:9)
                 "That if thou shalt confess with thy mouth the Lord Jesus, and shalt believe in thine heart that God hath raised him from the dead, thou shalt be saved."

Evangelist: If you confess the Lordship of Jesus and know deep in your heart that God raised Him from the grave you can be save. In other words you accept that free gift of salvation. You are saved from Hell, Saved for Heaven but most importantly you are save to have a relationship with Jesus Christ starting right now. And this gift is for everyone look at this: (Romans 10:13) "For whosoever shall call upon the name of the Lord shall be saved." Does that mean you Joe? (Wait for response). Does that mean you Glen? (Wait for response). That means everyone.

                 I'm sure glad you both came in today. Do you mind if I have a quick word of prayer with you before you go?

Joe, Glen: Okay.
Evangelist: Dear Lord, thank you for allowing Joe and Glen to come into the tent today, I thank you that they listened to your plan of salvation and I pray that your Holy Spirit has been dealing with their hearts as they heard your word. Now, fellas, if you would

like to accept Jesus as your Savior today I invite you
to say these words after me. Just say,
(begin this sinner's prayer allowing the person to
repeat after you)
'Dear, Lord….(pause)
I know that I am a sinner…(pause)
I accept Jesus as my Savior…(pause)
I believe you raised Him from the Dead…(pause)
Lord thank you for saving me…(pause)
Amen…

That's all there is to it. Now you're a child of God.
Your name is written in the Lamb's Book of Life and
you have found the true way to heaven which is
through Jesus Christ, our Lord.

What I would like for you to do now is fill out this
prayer card. At the end of the day we pray for all the
people who have accepted Jesus as their Savior.

And I would also like you to take this short flyer that
explains what you should do next.

It's important to remember that due to federal law it is illegal to collect
personal information from anyone under the age of 14 without parent
permission.
There are two purposes for the prayer cards, the first being the
most important, to pray for the new convert. When you read through
the prayer requests some will make your heart break. At the end of the
evening before shutting down, it is suggested the workers gather and
pray over the cards. Second, it is so the sponsoring church can follow
up on the new converts. It is important not to push the new convert
into giving more information than they want to share so that they do
not think you have ulterior motives for being at the fair.
It is also good at this time to put something in the hands of the
new believers; Inside the Box gives all new converts a copy of the
Gospel of John and Romans, and a tract that includes the name, phone
number and contact information of the sponsoring church. The leaflet
also has the address and phone number of the sponsoring church on the
back. IBFM has also put together a booklet that should be handed out

entitled, "Now What Do I Do?" (Appendix 6-6e).

APPENDIX 6 : Leaflet, "Now What Do I Do?"
This is an 8 ½ x 11 flyer folded into four panels. Due to size constraint and for legibility we have broken it into 5 sections here placed in the order in which it is read. The column layout position is indicated above each section. A sample of the flyer or a PDF is available just by asking.

COVER : Front Column 2:

NOW
WHAT DO
I DO?

Seek ye first the kingdom
of God...Matt 6:33

Answers for the
New Christian

APPENDIX 6a : Leaflet, Front Columns 3 & 4

AS A NEW CHRISTIAN WHAT SHOULD I DO NEXT?

- Be Baptized
- Read your Bible daily
- Pray regularly
- Become part of a local Bible-believing church
- Tell others about Christ

WHAT DOES IT MEAN TO BE BAPTIZED?

Jesus established the church, "...*Upon this rock I will build my church*" (Matthew 16:18) "...*Christ also loved the church, and gave himself for it,*" (Ephesians 5:25).When a person comes to Christ they immediately become part of His Church.

Ordinances are the things Jesus told us to observe. In the Church there are two ordinances, the first is baptism, the second is the Lord's Supper. The ordinance of biblical baptism is done through immersion. The word 'baptism' in the original Greek means "to plunge," in this case, into water. It is symbolic of a person's burial and death in Christ as well as their resurrection in Him (Romans 6:4). Although many people may have been "baptized" as infants, true baptism, as practiced in the Bible, comes only after a person comes to know Jesus as their Savior (Acts 2:41, Acts 8:36, 37). Baptism is considered an ordinance because Christ ordered all who come to Him to do so

Recommended Bible Reading on Baptism: Acts 8:26-40 Pay special attention to verses 36 and 37.

Bible Memory verse on being Baptized " *If ye love me, keep my commandments.*" (John 14:15).

HOW DO I COMMUNICATE WITH GOD?

In order for God to have an impact in the lives of believers He setup two means of communicati we can interact.

- He speaks to us Word (the Bible).
- We speak to God through prayer.

THE BIBLE The Bible is the inspired, infallible word of God. (2 Timothy 3:16-17) As we read God's Word the Holy Spirit guides us to its meaning (1 Corinthians 2:13). This is because the same Holy Spirit was the author of all scripture (2 Timothy 3:16). A daily time of devotion needs to be the habit of every believer. Make it a habit to rise early and begin the day with God. God's word has the answer for every problem we face in life

Memory Verse on the Bible: "Thy word have I hid in mine heart that I might not sin against thee." (Psalm 119:11).

Bible Tips to follow:

- The Bible is a believer's friend. Take it with you.

APPENDIX 6b: Leaflet, Rear Columns 1 & 2

PRAYER The Lord Jesus is our example in prayer. He arose early to spend
time in prayer. (Mark 1:35) He
left the crowds and spent time
alone with God in prayer (Mark
6:46). Another time to pray is
before meals (at home or in public)
and before you go to bed at night.
Pray whenever and wherever the
need arises (1 Thessalonians 5:17). We
become more effective in prayer as we
pray more.

A new Christian's first prayers
may be as simple as asking God for
daily strength, to meet their needs,
and for the salvation of friends and
loved ones. The believer will grow in
the Word of God and their prayer life
will draw them into a more intimate,
personal relationship with God, who
will reveal himself and his plans
(Jeremiah 33:3).

Bible Memory Verse on Prayer

"If ye abide in me, and my words abide
in you, ye shall ask what ye will, and it
shall be done unto you." (John 15:7).

WHAT PURPOSE DOES THE CHURCH SERVE?

When a person receives the Lord in
their heart, they are saved and become part of Christ's greater Church,
or what many refer to as, the family of
God. A local church is made up of a
group of saved, baptized believers
who have freely joined together to
carry out what is referred to as the
Great Commission: "Go ye therefore,

and teach all nations, baptizing them in
the name of the Father, and of the Son,
and of the Holy Ghost: Teaching them to
observe all things whatsoever I have commanded you: and, lo, I am with you always, even unto the end of the world.
Amen." (Matthew 28:19-20).

WHAT CAN I DO FOR MY CHURCH?

Be a Praying Member of Your
Church: Pray for the leaders and the ministries and activities. Pray for the members
and their needs.

Be a Loyal and Faithful Member of
Your Church: Be loyal to the leadership,
the worship services and the
ministries of the church. Lead
by Christ's example and encourage others to do the
same. Promote unity in the
Church by not complaining. With a cheer-
ful heart, every member of the local
church should do all they can to support
their church and all God wants it to be. If
it were not for local churches, most people would not hear what they must do to
be saved.

HOW CAN I LEAD SOMEONE TO CHRIST?

Personal Soul Winning When someone
comes to the Lord they are then given the
responsibility to tell others how to be
saved. The best place for a new Christian
to begin witnessing is to their closest
friends and dearest loved ones. Every new
believer in Christ should start telling the
good news of Jesus immediately.

Christ Will Save the Lost There is no one

APPENDIX 6d: Leaflet, Rear Columns 3 & 4

so lost that Christ cannot save him. He will save anyone who calls on Him for salvation (Romans 10:13). Although you may be timid at first, remember it is Jesus that does the saving. Be confident in His ability to supply you with the right words.

Begin By Telling Your Story A testimony is telling a personal experi-ence. When we tell others what Christ has done for us it allows others to relate first hand. To help you in relating your testimony, take a few prayerful moments and ask the Lord to help you write in the following information that you can share with the lost.

1. My life before receiving Christ was. . .

2. I came to know Christ when. . .

3. Now that I am saved what Christ means to me is. . .

WHAT DOES IT MEAN TO BE SAVED?

Next share with someone the steps to being saved as reviewed here.

When a person is 'saved' they are saved from sin (Mark 2:1-11, Matthew 26:28, 1 John 1:7). However, salvation goes beyond just having our sins forgiven. The word 'saved' or 'salvation' means *"To be delivered, to be preserved, to be made safe."* When a person is saved they are also

- delivered from Hell (Luke 16:19-31, Revelation 21:8)
- preserved for Heaven (John 14:1-6).
- saved to have a relationship with God right now (Romans 8:15, Galatians 4:6).

This only happens if a person has Christ in their heart.

HOW AM I SURE CHRIST IS IN MY HEART?

Christ died for our sins and wants to save everyone (2 Peter 3:9). However, God will not force His salvation on anyone; a person must ASK God to be saved. At the moment we do, Jesus comes into our heart, forgives our sins and saves our soul. We become a child of God (John 1:12), a new creation (2 Corinthians 5:17) and our name is written in the Book of Life (Revelation 21:27).

LET'S REVIEW

Q1:From what does Jesus save us? From our sins, (Mark 2:1-11, Matthew 26:28, 1 John 1:7).

Q2: What is sin? Sin is anything that displeases God (1 John 3:4).

Q3: Who has sinned? *"All have sinned..."* (Romans 3:10, 23).

Q4: What is the penalty for sin? Eternal or Spiritual death [Hell]. (Romans 6:23).

Q5: How can someone be saved from this death? They can be saved from eternal death by accepting Jesus as their Savior, (Acts 16:31).

Q6: How do you ask? By FAITH, call upon God, confess with your mouth the Lord Jesus, and believe in your heart that God raised him from the dead and you will be saved. (Romans 10:9, 13).

APPENDIX 6e: Leaflet, Front Column 1

Recommended Bible Reading: 1 John, 5   Read it once, then go back and reread it and underline or highlight the verses which talk about eternal life and how we can be sure God gives us this life through the Lord Jesus Christ.

Bible Memory verse on Assurance of Salvation: *"These things have I written unto you that believe on the name of the Son of God; that ye may know that ye have eternal life, and that ye may believe on the name of the Son of God."* (1 John 5:13).

Inside The Box Fair
Ministry
2933 Frembes Rd.
Waterford, MI 48329
(248) 812-FAIR

 Inside the box fair ministry

 Boxfairministry

BIBLIOGRAPHY

Amazing Grace Missions. *Our History: Amazing Grace Missions*. Dayton, TN, 2012. http://www.agm-ffci.org/ourhistory.asp (accessed September, 2012).

Anfuso, Francis. "Are You Going to Heaven." *Christian Equippers International*, 1981.

Bearing Precious Seed. Bibles. http://www.bpsmilford.org/ (accessed March, 2013).

Children Evangelism Fellowship. About Us. http://www.cefonline.com/index.php?option=com_content&view=section&id=8&Itemid=100032 (accessed September, 2012).

Children Evangelism Fellowship of Michigan. Fairs and Festivals. doi:www.cefmi.com/Fairs.shtml, Aug. 19, 20012 (accessed August, 2012).

Dictionary, Encarta. *Barker*. London: Microsoft Publishing, 2012.
———. *Entertain*. London: Microsoft Publishing, 2012.

Foxe, John. *Foxe's Book of Martyrs*. Cedar Rapids, Iowa: Parsons Technology,, 1999.

Full Gospel Men's Fellowship San Diego. The History of the Godmobile. http://www.godbiz.com/god-mobile (accessed September, 2012).

Ham, Ken. *The Lie*. Green Forest, AR: Master Books, 2012.

Highland, Jim. Growing A Giving Church. http://www.youtube.com/watch?v=oDnVzgxyZfE (accessed October, 2012).

Hoke, Donald E. *Revival in Our Time*. Wheaton, IL: Van Kampen Press, 1950.

Jenkins, Paul. History of the Godmobile Ministry.
http://www.godbiz.com/wp-content/uploads/2011/06/The-History-of-the-God-Mobile.pdf (accessed September, 2012).

Mims, Gene. *The Kingdom Focused Church*. Nashville, TN: B&H
Publishing, 2003.
———. The Kingdom Focused Church Seminar.
http://www.youtube.com/watch?v=XGKB-OlLcBU (accessed
November, 2012).

Rudloe, Jack. Gulf Specimen Marine Laboratory. gulfspecimen.org
(accessed October, 2012).

Slattery, Dean, and Slattery. "Are You Going to Heaven?" *Salvation
Tract*, 2010.

Stott, John. *Basic Christianity*. Donors Grove, IL: Intervarsity Press, 2008.
Strong, Augustus H. *Systematic Theology*. Philadelphia, PA: American
Baptist Publication Society, 1909.

Wikipedia. Benz, Karl. http://en.wikipedia.org/wiki/Karl_Benz (accessed
August, 2012).
———. Ford, Henry. http://en.wikipedia.org/wiki/Henry_Ford (accessed
August, 2012).
———. Olds, Ransom. http://en.wikipedia.org/wiki/Ransom_Olds
(accessed August, 2012).

REVIEW OF LITERATURE

Following is a review of the literature, grouped by category, used in the writing of this work.

History of Evangelism:
"Foxe's Book of Martyrs," by John Foxe, Parsons Technology, Inc. Cedar Rapids, Iowa, 1999.

This classic work needs to be in every person's library. This work was used to investigate the persecution of the early church and its effect on evangelism throughout the church age.

"Evangelism and the Remaking of the World," Adna Wright Leonard, The Methodist Book Concern, New York, 1919.

This book is a good source to assist a pastor in preaching and teaching evangelistic messages. Not a good source for evangelizing outside the church. Was not referenced in this work.

"Evangelism in the Early Church," Michel Green. Michel Green Publishing, Grand Rapids Mi, 2003.

The book was used to understand the early evangelistic methods employed by the early church fathers, why the church went underground and how evangelism became more personal and secretive in nature to help secure the safety of the early Christians. Well written.

History of Modern Market Place Evangelism:
"Our History," Amazing Grace Missions, Dayton, Tn. http://www.agm-ffci.org/ourhistory.asp.

This website is informative in telling the history of Amazing Grace Missions. It also helps to understand this ministry's mission and how they reach the lost.

"History of the Godmobile Ministry," Paul Jenkins, San Diego Ca., 2012, http://www.godbiz.com/wp-content/uploads/2011/06/The-History-of-the-God-Mobile.pdf.

This website reports the early history of the Godmobile ministry.

"Full Gospel Men's Fellowship San Diego Ca, Chapter 1881," Web page, http://www.godbiz.com/god-mobile.
  This website helps the visitor to understand the method this ministry uses to bring people to the saving grace of Jesus.

"About Us, Children Evangelism Fellowship," Warrenton Mo 2012, http://www.cefonline.com/index.php?option=com_content&view=section&id=8&Itemid=100032.
  This website explains the mission and ministry of Children Evangelism Fellowship.

"Fairs and Festivals, Children Evangelism Fellowship of Michigan, Lansing mi. 2012," http://www.cefmi.com/Fairs.shtml, Aug. 19, 2012.
  This website showed where the Michigan branch of Children Evangelism Fellowship had been over the past few years and the salvation results of their efforts.

Surveys and Tracts Used in Fair Ministry:
"Are You Going To Heaven?" Dean Slattery, Ionia Mi.
  This is a survey tract used by many of the Full Gospel Men's Fellowship's Godmobile. Though used in fair settings it can also be used in a church's regular evangelism program. It is a very well written tract. I have personally seen people come to the Lord simply by reading this work.

"Are You Going to Heaven?" Francis Anfuso, Christian Equippers International, (1981).
  This is a survey tract used at fairs and festivals. Another well written tract bountifully supplied with scripture reference and explanation. It can also be used by the individual to accept salvation.

Statistical Research:
"The Lie," Ken Ham, Master Books, Green Forest Ark, 2012.
  Ken Ham's classic work on the defense of creation as seen in the book of Genesis, used in this work to help the changing face of America today from a religious society to a secular one.

"Revival in Our Time," Donald E. Hoke, Van Kampen Press, Wheaton, Illinois, 1950.

Book shows the early history of the Billy Graham crusades. Was used in this work for statistical information on number of church member that were saved at Graham crusades.

"Growing A Giving Church Lecture," Dr. Jim Highland, Newburg Theological Seminary, Newburg Ind.

Statistical information used to show decline of church attendance in the U.S. population between the ages of thirteen and twenty-six.

ABOUT THE AUTHOR

Dr. Thomas Miller, has been pastor of First General Baptist Church of Waterford, Michigan for 16 years. His wife, Laura, also serves with him and is an author/illustrator in ministry for children. They have two daughters and four grandchildren.

Dr. Miller has a passion for winning souls and teaching others the joy of leading the lost to Jesus. He is available for speaking and soul winning training sessions.

His degrees and affiliations include:
B.R.E., M.R.E. Midwestern Baptist College, Pontiac, MI
M. Min., Master's Divinity School, Evansville, IN.
D. Min., Newburgh Theological Seminary, Newburgh, IN.
Pastor: First General Baptist Church, Waterford, Mi. (1997- Present).
School Administrator: Waterford General Baptist Academy, Waterford MI., (2000-2011)
Chief Administrator and Instructor: Waterford Bible Institute, Waterford Mi. (2002-2010)
Co-director: Inside the Box Fair Ministry, Waterford, Mi. (2008-present).

Please contact Dr. Miller at any time with questions, news and updates regarding this ministry. To God be the Glory.

Email: revtompastor@msn.com
Phone: (248) 812-FAIR (3247)

ENDNOTES

[1] Ken Ham, *The Lie* (Green Forest, AR: Master Books, 2012), 160.

[2] Donald E. Hoke, *Revival in Our Time* (Wheaton, IL: Van Kampen Press, 1950), 46.

[3] Jim Highland, Growing A Giving Church, http://www.youtube.com/watch?v=oDnVzgxyZfE (accessed October, 2012

[4] Jack Rudloe, Gulf Specimen Marine Laboratory, gulfspecimen.org (accessed October, 2012).

[5] John Foxe, *Foxe's Book of Martyrs* (Cedar Rapids, Iowa: Parsons Technology,, 1999), 8-10.

[6] Amazing Grace Missions, *Our History: Amazing Grace Missions* (Dayton, TN, 2012), http://www.agm-ffci.org/ourhistory.asp (accessed September, 2012).

[7] Paul Jenkins, History of the Godmobile Ministry, http://www.godbiz.com/wp-content/uploads/2011/06/The-History-of-the-God-Mobile.pdf (accessed September, 2012).

[8] Full Gospel Men's Fellowship San Diego, The History of the Godmobile, http://www.godbiz.com/god-mobile (accessed September, 2012).

[9] Dean Slattery, "Are You Going to Heaven?," *Salvation Tract*, 2010, 3.

[10] Francis Anfuso, "Are You Going to Heaven," *Christian Equippers International*, 1981, 11.

[11] Children Evangelism Fellowship, About Us, http://www.cefonline.com/index.php?option=com_content&view=section&id=8&Itemid=100032 (accessed September, 2012).

[12] Children Evangelism Fellowship of Michigan, Fairs and Festivals, doi:www.cefmi.com/Fairs.shtml, (accessed August, 2012).

[13] Ibid.

[14] Wikipedia, Benz, Karl, http://en.wikipedia.org/wiki/Karl_Benz (accessed August, 2012).

[15] Wikipedia, Olds, Ransom, http://en.wikipedia.org/wiki/Ransom_Olds (accessed August, 2012).

[16] Wikipedia, Ford, Henry, http://en.wikipedia.org/wiki/Henry_Ford (accessed August, 2012).

[17] Figures based on information from 2012 prayer cards.

[18] Encarta Dictionary, *Barker* (London: Microsoft Publishing, 2012).

[19] Encarta Dictionary, *Entertain* (London: Microsoft Publishing, 2012).

[20] John Stott, *Basic Christianity* (Donors Grove, IL: Intervarsity Press, 2008), 25.

[21] Annual Business Meeting reports when available, 1957-2007.

[22] Inside The Box Fair Ministry Statistical Information

[23] Augustus H. Strong, *Systematic Theology* (Philadelphia, PA: American Baptist Publication Society, 1909), 3:890.

[24] Gene Mims, *The Kingdom Focused Church* (Nashville, TN: B&H Publishing, 2003), 131.

[25] Gene Mims, *The Kingdom Focused Church Seminar*, http://www.youtube.com/watch?v=XGKB-OlLcBU (accessed November, 2012).

[26] Bearing Precious Seed, Bibles, http://www.bpsmilford.org/ (accessed March, 2013).

[27] Shakespeare William , *As You Like It, Act I scene1*

[28] Stongs Greek Lexicon, Public Domain, #G2288

Made in the USA
Middletown, DE
21 June 2022

67527009R00055